COLLECTIVE
DISRUPTION

COLLECTIVE DISRUPTION

HOW CORPORATIONS & STARTUPS
CAN CO-CREATE **TRANSFORMATIVE** NEW BUSINESSES

MICHAEL DOCHERTY

To Luc,
A fellow Innovator !
Keep it up !
Best Regards

POLARITY PRESS
BOCA RATON, FL

Published by
Polarity Press
Boca Raton, FL

Publisher's Cataloging-in-Publication Data
Docherty, Michael.

Collective disruption : how corporations and startups can co-create transformative new businesses / by Michael Docherty. – Boca Raton, FL : Polarity Press, 2015.

p. ; cm.

ISBN13: 978-0-9860795-0-4

Business planning. 2. Strategic planning. 3. New business enterprises—Planning. 4. Management—Technological innovations. 5. Business incubators. 6. Entrepreneurship. I. Title.

HD30.28.D63 2015
658.4012—dc23   2014959227

FIRST EDITION

Project coordination by Jenkins Group, Inc.
www.jenkinsgroupinc.com

Interior design by Brooke Camfield
Illustrations by Paul Grech

Printed in the United States of America
19   18   17   16   15   •   5   4   3   2   1

CONTENTS

Visit www.collectivedisruption.com for enhanced content, free tools, and recommended resources to help you apply collective disruption principles in your own business.

INTRODUCTION

Years ago, when I joined Sunbeam Corporation as VP of product development, the company was in shock and in crisis. Reeling from the effects of its brutal ex-CEO (the infamous "Chainsaw Al" Dunlap) and mired in bankruptcy, Sunbeam needed to rebuild its ability to innovate. Quickly.

As part of the turnaround team, we set about restoring the process of collaboration internally. But, clearly, that would not be enough. For a company in bankruptcy, we had no choice but to learn how to leverage outside experts in areas such as product development. We didn't call it open innovation, but that's what it was. We partnered with suppliers, inventors, and outside companies like never before. We went from launching 10 new products in the first year to more than 150 by the end of the second. And you know what? Working with these creative partners actually made us more creative thinkers inside the company. Our management team navigated Sunbeam through a Chapter 11 reorganization, rebuilt the business, and returned it to profitability. A few years later, Jarden Corporation acquired the business.

That was my introduction to the concept of open innovation. The experience took me in a new direction in my work and helped inform the business evolution I've championed in my ventures and with my clients.

I've spent 10 years leading a boutique consulting practice (Venture2) and working with large companies and startups in open innovation—connecting, collaborating, and commercializing innovations. I've also run venture-funded startups and worked for a venture capital firm investing in open innovation platforms during this period. I've experienced open innovation from many perspectives. Open innovation to support the core business is important, but it isn't enough.

The old definition of innovation is dead. The process that companies used to follow of innovating a new product or a new iteration on an existing brand is just what it takes to stay alive these days. In this highly connected world, new ideas are coming from everywhere, with emerging competitors disrupting established companies every day. Companies need to increasingly focus on new business creation for step-change growth. This is scary because transformative innovation is not what most big companies are good at. This book addresses that soft spot in the big-company skill set. I'm teaching the art of collaboration for new business creation.

Companies must learn to play the disruption game and use it to continually reinvent themselves. The time has come to challenge the paradigm that the startups are always the ones that disrupt large, established companies. Through the collective disruption model, you can engage and leverage the entrepreneurial ecosystem to co-create new market-disrupting businesses.

Collective disruption combines the best of big brands and startup nation.

Let me confess upfront that the word "disruption" (which you'll see in these pages) is an overused one. In this book, I'll be referring to disruptive innovation in a slightly broader sense than Clayton Christensen's traditional definition: disrupting a market via a technology or solution that brings simplicity and affordability and typically serves an unattractive niche within the market before it eventually redefines the industry. So, I'll more frequently refer to transformative innovation. Whatever label we give it, I'm addressing the type of innovation that can redefine companies and industries and is about helping to transform companies by creating whole new businesses or growth platforms. Transformative innovation by my definition is therefore not sustaining or core business innovation aimed at maintaining today's business.

If you're an executive in a large company, charged with growth through transformative innovation, this book is for you. You may be a GM or a leader in marketing, business development, R&D, or perhaps a dedicated group focused on new business creation. You're living the unique challenge of creating transformational and step-change growth in a company that rewards stability and optimization. While corporate innovation like this is difficult, there's no shortage of passion within the leaders and teams at companies I work with. The challenge is how to unleash it in ways that aren't stamped down by the cultures, reward systems, and policies of these companies. I've had the great experience of being in your shoes and working alongside visionary corporate leaders who are tackling these challenges.

I've also had the rewarding opportunity of being an entrepreneur, founding a venture-funded startup, and then becoming president of an early-stage venture capital firm. So if you're an entrepreneur or startup founder, I hope to provide insights for you as well. While I'll be speaking mostly to the corporate leader in this book, entrepreneurs can gain answers on how to partner with corporations in new ways and how they can leverage corporate partners to reverse engineer their businesses for faster scale-up and exit.

This book introduces the concept of the innovation ecosystem, its presence, its power, and the ways in which companies of all sizes can become connected in order to meet the demands of the new innovation imperative. In the following chapters we'll address:

- Why big companies are being left behind in the new hyper-fast innovation game

- How an innovation ecosystem can help companies create not just new products but also entirely new lines of business

- How the entrepreneurial skills of lean startups can (and can't) be applied in the corporate environment

- How a co-innovation strategy—with entrepreneurs and corporations—yields new business creation faster and at a lower risk

- New approaches to business incubation that leverage the best of entrepreneurial and corporate skills in prove-out and scale-up

- What skills are needed to manage this co-creation process for the profitability and success of all involved

In the first part of the book, I'll focus on how the innovation game is changing and how it's playing out across big and small companies. I'll look at the difficulties large companies are having in generating and implementing big new ideas and how entrepreneurs may hold the solution. I'll discuss open innovation and its much-needed evolution from transactional approaches to more relationship-based networks. This isn't another book on open innovation, but that foundation is important for my premise: that large companies and startups can co-create transformative new businesses.

In the second part, I'll look ahead to the ways in which collaboration and co-creation can be harnessed for new business creation and transformative innovation. Adapting lessons from venture capital firms and the lean startup movement, I'll detail the ways in which large companies can embrace this ecosystem concept and move forward and make it a reality. Companies are finding new ways to incubate businesses by bringing entrepreneurs and startups into their businesses or moving transformational innovation to the outside via accelerators and other models. I'll introduce a framework that takes you from discovery to scale-up and integration of these strategic growth initiatives.

Throughout this book, I'll share case studies and interviews with leaders in this collective disruption revolution from large companies, accelerators, and entrepreneurial firms. These executives speak candidly about the challenges and opportunities they've faced in bringing big ideas to life.

We've entered a new era of innovation, for entrepreneurs and big companies alike—the era of the collective disruption. I invite you to join in, understand the rules of this new game, and learn how to play to win.

PART 1:

THE GAME HAS CHANGED

1

THE ERA OF DISRUPTION

Once upon a time, there was a company whose name was synonymous with innovation.

Eastman Kodak could lay claim to some of the most creative and enduring innovations of the twentieth century. Kodak led the development of film-based photography, and scarcely a consumer in the marketplace went untouched by the revolution. It was the company that gave us the Brownie, Kodachrome, the Instamatic. So entwined with photography did this company become that its very name became the phrase we used to describe a cultural touch point: "a Kodak moment." By the 1970s, Kodak controlled a whopping 90% market share of photographic film sales in the United States and had the profits to match.

Yet, by 2012, the icon would be in bankruptcy.

What happened?

The digital revolution arrived, and Kodak failed to adapt. It wasn't for lack of trying. Kodak was fully aware of its predicament even as it emerged, worsened, and then became a full-blown crisis. Many attempts were made internally to respond to the massive change that digital technology brought to the photography market. Kodak restructured, it pledged to meet the challenge of the digital age, and it exhorted its innovation teams to focus in this new direction.

The Kodak story goes beyond the obvious point that it missed the shift to digital cameras. Author Haydn Shaughnessy in his book *Shift* makes the case that the real disruption for Kodak was mobile phones and our changing photography habits. Interestingly, Kodak owned significant mobile camera technology (CMOS) and even display technology, but wasn't able to capitalize on it.

In the end, the business could not make the leap into a transformed market. The beloved brand slid into financial ruin.

In many ways, the Kodak story is one that exemplifies the need for this book: a company was born, grew, and thrived on new inventions and then, once large, found itself unable to adapt that innovation process within its successful framework. Kodak didn't turn its back on innovation; indeed, company officials continued to beat the drum for innovation throughout the decline. Still, it was a company that could not seem to recapture its innovative streak. Cut off from its creative wellspring, it eventually was starved out of the business it had once dominated—even, arguably, invented.

The situation that Kodak faced is not unique. Big companies—once innovative companies—are experiencing it over and over again. Think about RIM and its rapid fall from grace as it missed the smartphone revolution and refused to reinvent itself in the exploding consumer market for these phones and the ecosystem of apps that they spawned. Think about the ongoing disruption of the publishing industry. The *New York Times* itself created a telling internal report (which was later made public) on the challenges of the digital revolution and a call to action to do more—faster—or die. Not long after the report was drafted in April 2014, the *Times* ousted its executive editor, and the incoming replacement, Dean Baquet, wrote in an internal e-mail to staffers: "The best companies constantly look for ways to get better. They embrace change, rather than simply telling themselves how good they are. As great as we are journalistically, there is much more to be done digitally."

This story will continue to be told about those who fail to adapt and embrace the new definition of innovation and its now-necessary connection to new business creation. The old definition of innovation is dead. Just ask Kodak and the many, many other big brands that find themselves caught in this transition. According to research by Richard Foster (author of *Creative Destruction*), the average tenure of companies in the S&P 500 has shrunk from 61 years back in 1958 to just 18 years as of 2012. At this rate, 75% of the current S&P 500 will be replaced by 2027. Another study (by Stubbart and Knight) showed that less than 1% of firms live to age 40. Companies must reinvent themselves or die.

This crisis is personal to me. I have been on both sides of the conference table as it has unfolded. In my work inside and outside of big brands, I have come to know, respect, and work alongside the managers who have to make innovation work for both the company and the customer. Theirs is a serious challenge. I know because it has been and continues to be mine as well.

Over the course of this book, I'll explore how to resolve this challenge on a large company scale by embracing more transformative approaches to growth. I'll go into great detail about the kind of new partnerships and new business creation orientation big companies need to adopt in order to regain the necessary innovation engine—the driving force that unless restarted will simply let a company sputter into bankruptcy or has-been status.

But for this chapter, I'll focus on the why, because it's a reasonable and important question to address at this stage in our conversation. Why can't big companies seem to innovate and create new sources of growth? They should be able to do anything. They've got all the resources and connections and the deep bench of talent that tiny firms can only dream about. Amazing things should be possible. So when that doesn't happen—and it doesn't happen for lots and lots of big companies—it makes sense to step back and try to understand the forces that trip the mighty.

HOW THE GAME HAS CHANGED

One of the most important points to make at this juncture is this: it's not the company's fault. Which company? Any. I could list for you a dozen firms currently on the hot seat for having lost their innovative edge. It's a commonly told tale. As any company (RIM? General Motors? Sears?) struggles to come up with innovative new ideas, critics will often point to individual errors made by company management. Some of this criticism may be perfectly valid, but it misses a larger point. In our global economy today, we are experiencing a generalized trend of large companies struggling to harness innovation to drive new sources of growth. Something has happened that will not be fixed by company-specific finger-pointing.

In many ways, the problem that companies are experiencing starts at the very core of the innovation discussion—what we mean by "innovation." We use the word innovation to describe things that are new to the marketplace. Over many decades, we have learned to use the word "new" rather liberally. A change in packaging could qualify as new, as well as an update in formula, an additional flavor, even a move from family- to single-serving size. At one time, each of those things would qualify as innovation for many a successful company. "New and improved!" was the industry standard, and companies clearing this relatively low bar could count on retailers and consumers to respond positively and with wallets open. This was the old game (Fig. 1.1), when incremental core business innovation was enough to drive business growth.

THE OLD GAME

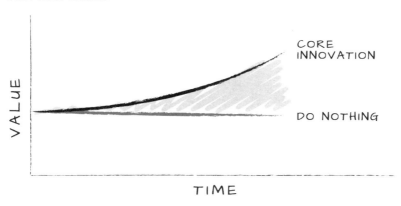

CORE
INNOVATION

DO NOTHING

VALUE

TIME

FIG. 1.1

Then came the digital revolution. Everything—including the definition of the word "innovation"—changed.

Technology underwent an expansion that rewired every industry. With the advent of the Internet, communications exploded in reach and in speed. A world that once relied on mail carriers and telephony was now hyper connected. People and companies could share ideas and collaborate on work at a higher and faster level than ever before.

With this technology boom came a blast of technology products onto the marketplace. In hardware, the parade of computers, desktops, laptops, cell phones, smartphones, and tablets was steady. The hardware came with a companion wave of software that erased barriers of time and distance. New services sprang up to serve this newly decked-out consumer with speed and precision. The technology changed the lives of millions.

It also changed our definition of what it meant to be innovative. In the new game (Fig. 1.2), core business innovation is what it takes to simply stay in the game. Revenue growth increasingly has to come from new sources and new platforms. Why?

THE NEW GAME

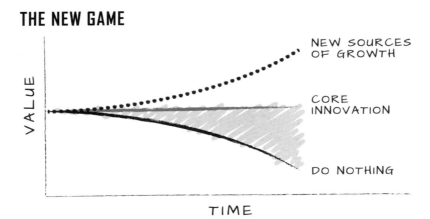

FIG. 1.2

Enthused by the groundbreaking, life-changing newness of the tech boom, end users at every level began to demand that rate of change on a regular basis. Consumers wanted to buy the new, exciting stuff. Retailers wanted to stock it. Stock analysts wanted to see this level of innovation in the pipeline of the companies they followed. Investors large and small scoured business plans not for slow, steady growth but for a breakout new product. Now, having something with a new color or new package wasn't enough; it had to be a new experience, a new idea, a breakthrough game changer. If not, it was ordinary. It paled in comparison to the exciting new tech stuff coming out of the startup communities all over the world. Now imagine as this level of expectation flows down to the folks who design cough syrup and toasters.

Every year, the unencumbered genius of the startup community produced some amazing new thing: maybe an even smaller way to house technology, an even faster way to communicate, an even richer entertainment experience. Standing next to the exciting newness of entrepreneurial experimentation, the innovation of many big consumer products companies started to look a bit stale. Think of it from the consumer perspective: if you had some cash to spend, what would catch your eye? The slightly new iteration on an old product you've known and loved forever or the fascinating, mind-blowing newness of the latest gadget or software?

Breakthrough and transformative innovation isn't new. What's new is the increasing dependence on this higher level of innovation for business growth. It's too easy to think of this shift as being one driven by technology—it was not just a question of new, faster machinery at work. What was happening in Silicon Valley and other centers of innovation, both real and virtual, was a new emergence of connectedness. Technology connected us in ways that were faster and more meaningful than ever before. Innovation wasn't what it used to be. The game had changed. Big companies were rapidly being left behind.

The shift was not lost on corporations. They may not have been first to spot it, but as it spread as a trend, they caught on. They knew the world had changed around them. In boardrooms up and down the Fortune 500, presentations were passionately made: *We need to be more innovative!* Many agreed this was necessary. No one argued against the need for better innovation. Yet few companies seemed to be able to actually do it.

How did this happen? The answer is complex; both external and internal forces drove the trend.

External Forces

The consumer marketplace has become a faster and more demanding game. Consumer products have to be better. Now that customers can shop across time zones, lesser products cannot run, and they cannot hide. Everyone—across all industries—is held to the highest standard. If in the old days customers might be satisfied with a mediocre product because that's all they knew to be available, today that veil is lifted. Today, they know immediately, with a click of the mouse, what is available to them and what the "best" in any given category might be. They're free to leave you for the better product at any time. And they will, too. This raises the bar for every company in a category. Consumer expectations have risen and show no signs of coming back down. This puts the pressure on companies to deliver products that meet the new higher standard.

Alongside the higher customer expectations comes a new demand for speed. If customers were once satisfied with an innovation every year or two, today that product cycle is vastly reduced. Companies find that their innovations are quickly copied and even overshadowed by competitors. The innovation game becomes one in which the innovators are constantly at a run, with little downtime between new product generations. Even as a new product or service debuts, already its challenger is entering the ring.

Fueling both of these trends—shorter product cycles and consumer expectations—is the broader trend of connectivity, not just in business but also in the human experience. We are all connected today in ways that were unimaginable a few years ago. We can know about retail trends in faraway lands. We can hear about breakthroughs around the world the day they happen. We can share our opinions and our experiences with clicks at light speed. Connectedness is not just a consumer phenomenon but also a phenomenon that has changed the company/ consumer relationship. Years ago, consumers might wish a product had a certain feature. Today, they'll fire up their mobile device and shoot the CEO an e-mail describing their demands—and they'll expect an answer. Connectedness is both a blessing and a curse for corporate entities. It allows companies to better understand what consumers want, and it is also an open channel through which consumers can talk back. That's not something Eastman Kodak had to worry about back in the Brownie days. Times have changed. Today, ideas come from everywhere.

Internal Forces

While those external forces were taking shape, companies were developing internal approaches that would ultimately stymie innovation efforts.

In fairness, big companies are not built to support breakthrough or transformative innovation. They are built to support optimization. The bigger any company grows, the more players extol its efficiencies, its economies of scale, its ability to replicate and execute on a wider stage. These are all processes that call for standards, best practices, rules, and regulations. They build companies that reward managers who can work within a system, not throw it into a tizzy with a lightbulb idea. Big companies prize the smooth, efficient running of their bigness, and the bigger they get, the harder it is to hold onto the disruptive energy of an innovative process. Big companies reward risk avoidance.

Here's a good example of that mindset at work. Years ago, the CEO of GE Capital wanted to jump-start the innovative energy of his company. So he offered two dozen of his managers an interesting opportunity: he pledged $1 million in funding to any of the managers who could take an idea and turn it into a new business. However, almost no one took the bait. Only one or two of the managers stepped forward to try. The rest were well wedded to the big-company mindset. Working on their own, they saw that known spaces seemed to offer more upside than taking a risk on a new approach—even with a $1-million incentive.

The GE Capital story is a classic rendition of the risk-averse mindset that pervades big companies. Sticking to what you know is better than risking something new, even if the payoff might be huge. With 22 out of 24 managers thinking this way, how could GE Capital hope to recapture its entrepreneurial mindset? Clearly, behaving in venture mode was far from attractive to the team leaders. But it's not an issue with individual employees. Rather, the culture and management behaviors that make these companies great at optimization stand in the way of disruptive thinking. When they try these "one-off" attempts such as that at GE Capital, few believe that it's real or that it's a long-term commitment.

There are many passionate and creative corporate leaders and employees. Udaiyan Jatar (U.J.), an experienced corporate innovator who now leads Blue Earth Network and its work in transformative innovation, told me: "I think we have a prejudice that big-company executives or employees are not creative. We also have this prejudice that they're not passionate, and these are wrong perceptions. They are very creative and very passionate. Just not passionate about incremental thinking—cost cutting and somehow trying to eke out a 0.2% growth in the quarter even when there may be disruptive, world-changing ideas that exist within those employees that are never tapped. The barriers to unleashing creativity are often self-inflicted and systemic, but they can be overcome and frequently are."

We need new ways to both unleash internal creativity and tap into external creativity sources for growth.

REBALANCING THE PORTFOLIO

Companies need growth. They need to find ways to create new business platforms while still managing and optimizing their current business. That's been the challenge of management for decades, if not centuries. The three-horizons framework originally presented in the book *The Alchemy of Growth* is a simple and proven framework for thinking about building a balanced portfolio of opportunities for today and for the future. What's changing is the pace at which companies need to replace these core products and businesses. That means more emphasis on creating options for future businesses. Figure 1.3 illustrates a three-horizon framework for growth

GROWTH HORIZONS

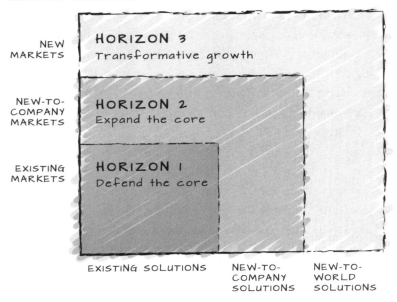

FIG. 1.3

Horizon 1: Defending and refreshing the core is where most companies spend their time and where most of today's revenues and profits come from. Ignore the core at your peril—I agree. However, what used to be growth from core business innovation is now what it takes just to stay in the game.

Horizon 2: Expanding the core and adding adjacencies are becoming much more important parts of the portfolio mix in today's hyper-competitive markets. The speed at which you need to identify and introduce these innovations and growth opportunities is accelerating. In many ways, rapidly introducing these opportunities is the new core strategy.

Horizon 3: Creating viable future options sometimes means monitoring and engaging in transformative innovation, which can involve market-disrupting opportunities. The payoffs are seldom in the short term, but the importance of this horizon to the future of the enterprise can't be understated, especially now that disruption is happening all around us on an almost daily basis. While still a smaller part of the portfolio mix, H3 work is more important now than ever, and yet many companies continue to focus on H1 and H2 almost exclusively. Why? Because H3 entails much more risk and is often much more about business model innovation than new products or services alone—precisely what large companies aren't historically good at and where they need the most help.

Companies need a balanced portfolio of initiatives across all three horizons. What's that ideal balance? It depends on your industry and your company's situation. But it's an important topic that the senior leadership team needs to address to understand the company's current focus and to set targets for the future. One study of a large cross section of companies (across industrial, technology, and consumer goods) conducted by Monitor (Deloitte) found that the high performers allocated their efforts/resources as follows: roughly 70% core, 20% adjacent, and 10% transformational. Google uses that same ratio as well. What's really interesting is that this same study showed that among high-performing companies, their distribution of returns was the reverse. Almost 70% of their total returns over time from innovation came from transformational innovation.

In a separate study of 1,700 CEOs conducted by IBM, underperformers (those companies with financial results below the average of the companies studied) were more focused on improving operations, while outperformers (those companies with financial results above the average) were more aggressively focused on business model innovation. For example, outperformers were 48% more likely to break into other industries and twice as inclined to invent entirely new ones. They also highlighted partnering as the key enabler in doing so. So while protecting the core remains job number 1, investing in transformational activities is the only way to survive for the long term.

Large companies are much more adept at H1 and H2 activities than they are at transformational (H3) initiatives. Startups live in this H3 space, and this is what makes them ideal partners for corporations in exploring and building them. Companies used to see H3 activities as very long term, which made it easier to de-prioritize versus nearer-term activities when times got tough. Today's startups are accelerating H3 activities at hyper speed, and companies need to engage now more than ever in these efforts.

SUSAN HARMAN,
VP & PRODUCT CHAMPION, LEXISNEXIS (FORMERLY WITH INTUIT)

Harman understands the importance and the challenge of pursuing new strategic opportunities in big companies. When we talked, she described the importance of breakthrough and long-term thinking, along with the need to explore opportunities quickly using entrepreneurial approaches.

Companies need to have a balanced portfolio. They need to grow and to grow strategically by entering either new markets or adjacent markets.

The problem I have observed in big companies over the years is keeping the momentum going. The challenge is that large companies have to balance revenue being generated by their H1 portfolio offerings and the investment required to investigate potential H3 offerings, because the moment the company has any type of revenue or profit challenge, the resources get pulled from the H3s over the years.

A challenge faced by H3 intrapreneurs is that large companies have operational systems and processes in place to support their H1 businesses, and, typically, those processes don't work for an H3. The H3 intrapreneurs are constantly faced with boulders in their path, and they have to figure out how to navigate around them, underneath them, over them—or blow them up.

So if a company does want to invest in an H3 portfolio, how does it get started? It should invest in a very small team—probably a seasoned product management leader paired with a marketing leader—and look for opportunities that are strategic, large market size, in a space that makes sense for the company to be in. The basic research is done pretty quickly just to decide, "Should we be exploring this space?"

That small team has to really dig into the target audience in order to really understand the customer problem to be solved and then follow the lean startup process that starts with identifying the most important hypothesis to prove true/false. It's about moving very quickly through the process. This should not be millions of dollars in investment and a year of R&D to determine whether this is a viable potential business. Instead, they are starting out very small by testing concepts with users to really determine whether there's a there, there—and then developing minimal viable functionality in order to solve for the love metrics and net promoter scores and not simply revenue and large user base.

It's basically minimal investment following lean principles to really just determine whether there is something there that the company should consider pursuing. The challenge is that, typically, they will find only one potential in 10 exploratory attempts. And that one potential might not generate revenue for years, and that is why companies often lose interest. One way to fast-track this is to partner with entrepreneurial companies that are in the space, but that too has its challenges with establishing the appropriate rules of engagement and expectations.

The reward is there if companies are patient. Intuit and LexisNexis recognize that it is a portfolio play, that it is a strategic and long-term focus, and that there might be only one home run out of many attempts.

Susan Harman is currently VP and product champion, LexisNexis. Prior to that, she was an innovation leader with Intuit. Harman is passionate about leading consumer-driven innovation, with a particular focus on whitespace opportunities.

THE MYTH OF THE AMBIDEXTROUS ORGANIZATION

Back in 2004, authors Charles O'Reilly and Michael Tushman made their case in a *Harvard Business Review* article for the ambidextrous organization. They argued that companies should be focused on developing strategies, cultures, and organizations that support both incremental innovation and discontinuous innovation. Around the same time, two other academics, Costas Markides and Paul Geroski, challenged that theory with a claim that the skills, mindsets, and competencies needed for breakthrough innovation were in conflict with those needed for mass-market optimization. They pointed out that few companies in the world were capable of sustaining both models and made the argument that large consolidator companies should acquire and scale the discontinuous innovations developed by pioneering firms. The debate continues among experts even today.

So which pair of authors was right? Neither and both.

The ambidextrous model has it right that companies must be able to orchestrate and deliver both incremental and transformational innovation for long term growth and success. The problem with the ambidextrous model is the assumption that a single company can successfully manage contradictory structures and processes in the same firm and do it all internally. Too few companies can pull this off. I would highlight 3M as one of the few exceptions to the rule here, capable of managing both incremental and transformative innovation within the same organization. Google is probably another. You might have some other companies in mind that are capable of being ambidextrous. However, the larger point here is that they are exceptions. From my experience working within large and successful companies, what makes these companies great at optimizing the current business makes them terrible at creating tomorrow's business.

The colonizer and consolidator model has it right that transformative innovation has to be about engaging external entrepreneurs. The problem is that the approach promotes a purely transactional M&A model for consolidation and misses the opportunity for earlier-stage collaboration instead of simply acquiring the innovation when it's scaling. Remember that when you're acquiring these startups in the later stages, they've already likely received significant venture capital, and these later-stage investors are typically looking for 10× or more back from their initial investment, so you'll be paying a premium if that's your only strategy for startup integration. Plus, you miss the opportunity to "reverse-engineer" startups by influencing their direction and aligning them toward your strategic goals and growth aspirations.

Sonny Jandial, a consultant with the Partnering Group who was previously one of Procter & Gamble's key liaisons in Silicon Valley, told me, "When you're also engaging in traditional M&A, you often hear 'Well, we can just buy these companies when they're ready to be scaled up, so why do we need this earlier engagement?' The benefit of having early relationships is that you can shape things. You can shape it into what's going to be the most impactful to facilitate the business side of it, while making sure that it's the right thing for consumer or user."

ARE YOU STUCK?

The world has no shortage of great ideas. What's often lacking is the ability or the will to act on them. Does your firm really have a problem following through on transformative innovation and new business opportunities? Note these key signs:

1. You're not growing. You may be turning out the same number of new products every year, but that method of innovation is just keeping you at base level. It's preventing a backward slide, but it's not growing your margins, and it's not growing your top line. Lack of growth is often a sign that you are stuck in incremental mode.

2. You're identifying needs to support today's business but are missing the major shifts with your customers and new segments of customers that you could have captured.

3. You've been surprised too often by disruptive solutions, sometimes introduced by your major competitors but increasingly by new players you've never even heard of.

4. Funding is over-allocated to incremental ideas at the expense of breakout ideas. Others may argue that you have some truly breakthrough projects on the drawing boards. Look at which projects in your innovation portfolio really get the support to come to fruition. Do you find that incremental ideas get a lot of support quickly while the breakthrough ideas stall, stay in a zombie state with no real financial support, or get killed off outright?

5. Management talks about innovation but doesn't really want it to happen. This can be a problem as high up as the C-suite. If company leaders are talking about transformative innovation but making no change in process or policy to support the new behavior, then it's just talk.

If this sounds like your company, don't panic. While the situation is challenging, the answer is out there. Big companies are usually terrible at risk taking and disruptive innovation. They need more than instruction on how to innovate in this new world. They need partners—partners who run toward risk with arms open wide, partners who haven't been around long enough to develop a canon of behavior that favors optimization over innovation. Big business needs to partner with entrepreneurs in new ways.

Traditionally, innovation has been an internal process. The creative minds of a company may have sequestered themselves deep in the corporate labs, away from the daily bustle of marketing or sales, cooking up new ideas that no one really understands until the team emerges to make the presentation to the rest of the firm.

But the days of the cloistered innovation team are long gone. Today, leaders in the corporate environment must redefine how they grow.

Procter & Gamble is learning how to compete in this new arena by continuing to innovate the core while exploring whole new business models that leverage their brands into new areas. In the old days, innovation meant "new and improved" Tide laundry detergent, perhaps with a new ingredient that enabled a claim of better whitening. More recently, P&G introduced Tide Pods, a very innovative product and enabling technology that reinvigorated the category. But even that isn't fueling significant growth for the brand. So now it is incubating whole new business models, including Tide-branded dry cleaners and Mr. Clean–branded car washes, in partnership with franchising experts as a way to leverage the brand into services far outside of its existing core. Time will tell whether this is a winning strategy. But P&G understands that it needs to try.

The opportunity is here for established companies to leverage startups and entrepreneurs as extensions of their organizations in new business creation. It's difficult enough to overcome the challenges to develop new products and services within your core, and it's nearly impossible to innovate entire new businesses and ventures where risks and unknowns are so much higher—unless you're willing to partner with those outside your company who specialize in just that way of thinking. This is not a prescription for an individual company with an individual problem; it is a mandate for industries ranging from consumer products to health care and industrial goods. The game has changed, so the players must change with it.

2

LESSONS FROM ENTREPRENEURS AND LEAN STARTUPS

Where does great innovation come from?

The answer to that question has evolved over time. It happened slowly but surely and left in its wake many brand managers scratching their heads and wondering how they ended up on the wrong side of the wall.

"Innovation" used to be synonymous with "big." Not long ago, the power and critical mass of a big company were key components for success.

Here's a famous example.

Bell Labs is a firm known for its innovative contributions to the business world, and it achieved those wins on far more than just luck and inspiration. Bell developed an innovation lab that became world-renowned. Its founder valued a strong sense of physical place, and the vast majority of R&D professionals worked out of the company headquarters.

The lab was designed to have offices off a long corridor, with the rule that doors to offices must always be kept open. To get from one area of the company to another, one had to travel the hallway and pass coworkers, visitors, and supervisors. This fostered communication and shared conversation. Research teams were funded and then left to their own imaginative devices; it was not unusual for a project to take years to go from idea to product. Researchers were set apart from the financial concerns of the firm. This system was spectacularly successful—through the twentieth century. After that, it began to lose its luster, with layoffs and a dismantling of the critical mass of in-house thinkers once considered vital to the lab's innovative processes. Bell Labs worked for so many years because it fostered innovation and collaboration. Now the speed of innovation and the locus of innovation were changing in the world around it.

Now here's a look at the kind of company that sprang up in Bell's wake.

In 2010, Stanford fellows Kevin Systrom and Mike Krieger launched a location service called Burbn. Similar to Foursquare, the program allowed users to check into locations, earn points for their actions online, and share pictures inside of the application.

Then, in the midst of their service's middling success, the creators opted to execute a move that characterizes success today: the pivot.

The cofounders made a shift within the context of their original idea, with a decision to focus on the photo-sharing actions of users. They added artsy filters for users to try. They offered more ways to share the photos more publicly, via social networks such Facebook and Twitter. The pivot paid off. The result was Instagram.

The pivot is just one element of entrepreneurial methods that corporate innovators can learn and adapt. I'll come back to this and other concepts later in this chapter.

ENTREPRENEURS: THE NEW VALUE CREATORS

The contrast between Bell and Instagram is instructive. It shows us how substantially the wellspring of innovation has relocated: it has shifted from the halls of big business to the coffee shops and garages of entrepreneurs. When you compare the output of traditional corporate innovation with that of the world of entrepreneurship, you can easily see that smaller firms are taking the lead by making creativity, speed, and risk taking a way of life. Because they offer a platform in which a pivot can happen, they are eclipsing the larger firms and are today's drivers of intellectual property and value creation. The challenge for large companies then becomes, can they find a way to tap into this world of startups and entrepreneurial innovation? Or has the evolutionary process already left them behind?

The numbers don't lie. Much of what is new and newly profitable today is churning out of the smaller emerging firms, not the Bell Labs.

According to the Kauffman Foundation, the number of high-tech firms created annually has increased 69% between 1980 and 2011. In the past five years, 70% of US job creation came from startups. Even during tough times, the entrepreneurial sector fairs better. Job creation for technology firms grew 11% between 1999 and 2011, compared with the shrinkage of 6% for all private firms. In those numbers, you can see the Bell Labs versus Instagram matchup. In the old days, you needed the bigness of an organization to make something new. Today, you are more likely to find that newness coming from a couple of students and their laptops.

In some areas, the contrast is even more striking. The Small Business Administration looked closely at the innovation trends around "green" business. The study found that small innovative firms are 16 times more productive than large innovative firms in terms of patents per employee. What's more, the green technology patents from small firms are cited 2.5 times as often as those of large firms in other patent applications, indicating that small firms' patents are more original and influential.

As I've mentioned, I know a lot of passionate and very talented innovators within big companies today. But these intrapreneurs often have an uphill battle as they continue to push the boundaries. Too often these folks end up leaving their corporations to become entrepreneurs themselves or to work for smaller, scrappier firms where these innovators can have more impact.

STARTUPS AS BEACONS

Large companies have a lot to learn from entrepreneurial firms, most especially related to their resiliency and ability to fight through difficulties. Here are some important lessons that large companies need to embrace in order to adopt more open and entrepreneurial approaches.

Give Up Control: The smartest people you need for your project may not work for you. They may never work for you. To tap into their genius, you will have to live with a collaborative work process that cedes some control. It's not the way most executives in large companies were raised, but it is the standard operating procedure of Silicon Valley and other entrepreneurial communities. To connect with these creatives, you need to be willing to play in a more flexible work environment than the traditional command-and-control one.

Bring Down All the Walls: Some of the best and brightest minds may reside outside your walls. Companies need to be encouraged to look outward from all departments, not just technology or R&D. The concept of cross-functional must be broadened to cross-organizational. As Larry Huston, P&G's Connect+Develop architect, wrote, "We needed to change how we defined and perceived our R&D organization—from 7,500 people inside to 7,500 *plus* 1.5 million outside, with a permeable boundary between them."

Don't Just Partner . . . Learn: Far too many big companies think all they need to do is reach out, find a good innovator in Silicon Valley, sign a contract, and let the project fly. The truth is the best outcomes in innovation are ones where the initial company not only has success in the marketplace with a new product but also learns to be a better innovator itself. The entrepreneurial companies can teach their new partners lessons, such as how to give up control for the greater good, how to connect and collaborate, and how to identify great ideas no matter where they originate. Perhaps most importantly, entrepreneurs can help big companies understand the difference between vision and tunnel vision. So many big companies are brought down by a practice they mistakenly see as a virtue: unwavering support for a goal or process. If you can't flex, then you can't win in today's marketplace. Entrepreneurs can teach and model the art of agility. You can maintain your goals and still have enough flexibility to handle twists and turns. Vision, but not tunnel vision—it's the difference between Facebook and MySpace.

Learning Goes Both Ways: Big companies can teach entrepreneurs and startups a lot as well. Branding, achieving scale, developing effective business strategies, appropriate discipline in business processes—the list goes on. Large companies may move more slowly, but many are truly learning organizations and have an ability to cross-fertilize ideas and lessons across large, complex businesses and widely dispersed teams. This is a partnership that's about leveraging the best of two different but complementary approaches. Who's learning and who's teaching depends on where you are in the process. The key is engaging earlier to allow for this.

THE LEAN STARTUP BLUEPRINT

How are the smaller firms able to churn out value while bigger firms stumble? One reason is the business practice known as lean startup methods, popularized by Eric Ries's book of the same name, which is a new idea to big companies but a way of life for many entrepreneurs today.

Lean startup approaches apply an iterative process termed "build-measure-learn" to take an idea from lightbulb moment to marketplace fruition. Far from the seat-of-the-pants imagery many have when it comes to entrepreneurship, the lean startup method prides itself on scientific process. Efforts are launched and measured. Data are gathered and processed so that they are instructive. Learning is validated at steps along the way so that a new idea doesn't just fly or crash but moves through the growth process in a systemic way.

The origins of lean come from lean manufacturing and much of it from the automotive industry. "Pull-through" systems to eliminate waste, just-in-time inventory, and real-time quality control feedback loops are all elements of lean manufacturing. My own background in lean comes from working at Ford Motor Company in product development, engineering, and manufacturing roles earlier in my career. The concept of lean is a powerful one, and I find it rewarding (and kind of funny) that my automotive experience is now actually helping me very directly in my work with corporate teams and startups in accelerating entrepreneurial ventures. I've been a strong believer in iterative development and in-market experimentation, well before the current lean movement took hold. I think it's a positive development that Eric Ries, as well as Steve Blank, Bob Dorf, and other pioneers of this movement, are championing these concepts in the world of startups and now corporate innovation teams.

I want to mention that the classic definition of "lean" is about removing variation and eliminating waste from manufacturing or business processes. This is important: innovation is not a linear or controlled process—it's anything but. So in the context of lean startup, we're talking about eliminating waste in a broader sense by conducting controlled early-stage experiments to learn quickly and iterate toward a solution. We're not going to eliminate variation from the innovation process and make it prescriptive, nor should we try.

Lean startup methods work because they take some of the guesswork and crossed fingers out of the innovation process. They encourage users to eliminate uncertainty and thereby work smarter, rather than harder, at the innovation process.

Those core concepts of lean thinking have launched a thousand startups—probably more than that. They comprise the bedrock process of the startup community.

LEAN FOR CORPORATES

The successes of the lean startup approach did not go unnoticed by the ranks of major enterprises.

As big companies struggled to innovate profitably, they watched with awe and envy as the little guys seemed to sprint with passion and fire through the innovation process and into the marketplace. They asked, how can we do that? The question was especially relevant since Ries and other early proponents of the system were so vocal in their belief that any company of any size could apply this kind of lean innovation.

Much can be applied, but to succeed, these large firms need to determine what can work for them and learn to partner with entrepreneurs on the outside whose risk profiles, organizations, and cultures are better suited for this extreme form of agility.

Can it work for the Big Guys? The answer is yes. The answer is not only yes but also yes and it's already happening. However, far too many big companies stumble when they attempt to apply lean startup principles, largely because they attempt to do it in a big-company way that is wholesale. That simply won't work.

The stumbles of some big companies don't mean that lean startup thinking is useless to the enterprise. Quite the opposite. Their instinct was right; it is the way forward. But instead of adopting lean methodologies wholesale, big companies must adapt the concepts so that they support and engage the enterprise.

One key difference defines big companies and startups: entrepreneurs are natural risk-takers. They have an agility and willingness to pivot in entirely new directions based on market feedback. Their time horizons for success within the venture capital model don't permit the luxury of time. On the other hand, large companies are, by their nature, risk averse. Their cultures, reward systems, and processes are based on optimizing brands, products, and delivery for business success at scale. Companies at scale cannot afford unnecessary risk taking. So when we take lean startup concepts into the big corporate setting, we have to do so with an understanding that discussions about risk will take place:

what it means; why it's necessary to the innovation process; and why lean startup concepts, adapted properly for the big enterprise, can actually mitigate risk.

Another important factor in adapting lean to the enterprise is recognizing the structural differences in companies developing complex products or services outside of a purely digital environment. Not that digital business models are simple, but the companies I work with in consumer products, consumer health care, and other industries face unique regulatory, safety, and quality requirements that inherently drive less ability to be nimble. No one wants a faulty or unsafe physical product in the hands of consumers.

That's where the need for adapting comes in. Lean has to be applied differently to meet the needs and parameters of the bigger firms.

Let's look at some of the key lean startup concepts. I'll go through each and how it can be adapted to work in a bigger company setting.

Customer Development: This is where lean thinking really does aim to eliminate waste in the startup process. Customer development is about "getting out of the building" to engage with customers directly and upfront, validating who customers are and what their problems are before undertaking significant product development.

Customer Development, Enterprise Style: Formal, sophisticated consumer and market research has its place, but for new breakthrough initiatives with high unknowns, put away the spreadsheets and get your teams outside of the building to engage directly with customers. There's great power in getting product or service development teams directly involved in upfront customer engagement. Simple contextual interviews in your customers' environment will invariably surface new insights that are then more deeply understood by development teams because they've heard them in the customers' own words. And simply searching for the right customers who fit your targeted profile is an early indicator for how hard it might be to find and reach these customers when you have a product or service to sell.

Example: When I was involved in supporting the development of a nanotechnology flow sensor with a client, the initial inclination was to develop a working prototype and pitch it to potential industrial companies in the market that my client assumed would be interested. Instead, we conducted interviews with executives in several different industries, from medical to industrial waste treatment. We did not focus on our solution but probed for which companies and industries were frustrated by the cost, inaccuracies, and size of current flow measurement technologies. These interviews drove a complete shift from an assumed focus on industrial flow sensors to more lucrative and whitespace opportunities for flow sensing in IV drips.

Validated Learning: Successful entrepreneurs develop new systems and products through a rigorous process of creating hypotheses and then testing these assumptions quickly to iterate toward a successful solution faster and at less expense. This build-measure-learn cycle repeats itself throughout development.

Validated Learning, Enterprise Style: This may be the easiest lean startup concept to translate from small company to big company. This is a discipline quite easily understood and adaptable to corporate venturing teams. Big companies love data. They hardly make a move without some sort of data. When I go into a big firm to talk about applying a validated learning experience, we help company leaders apply a phased approach to their programs with learning objectives at each stage. Lean startups' process of learning and applying that learning in an ongoing way is injected into existing big-company appreciation for numbers. The difference here is that we're measuring to learn and adjust, not just measuring against end goals.

Example: GlaxoSmithKline (GSK) used a series of defined experiments with limited funding to validate a breakthrough opportunity that entailed a new business model and disruptive solution for the consumer dentures market. According to Stan Lech, former VP of innovation, the team's ability to build-test-learn during definition of the project was a key factor in their speed and effectiveness.

Minimum Viable Product (MVP): Closely related to the concept of validated learning is building early versions of the product from the perspective of the absolute minimum needed versus the often traditional approach of providing many bells and whistles in the name of delivering additional value for the user/consumer.

MVP, Enterprise Style: By contrast, the MVP concept is often lost or misunderstood in a big-company setting. If you're developing a new drug or packaged good, the idea of MVP does not hold in a literal sense. We need to recognize that launching a software product that can be rapidly prototyped is a long way from a new drug being developed by a pharma company or a durable appliance that requires long-lead tooling. Instead, corporate teams need to create elements of the business proposition that can be developed and tested, usually in market. In the corporate context, MVPs need to be good enough to validate that your customers see the value and are willing to look past the initial flaws.

Example: Before the wonderful Tesla Model S was off the drawing boards, Elon Musk and the Tesla team developed and launched an MVP called the Roadster, which was, in essence, a Lotus Elise that was retrofitted with early-generation lithium ion battery packs. While still an expensive development effort, it provided invaluable performance and market feedback at a small fraction of the cost of a ground-up vehicle development program. I'll include more examples of MVPs for corporates in later chapters.

Pivot or Persevere: The build-measure-learn loop helps startups quickly get close to real customers and gain real-time feedback on needs. When done correctly, it will be clear whether the company is moving the drivers of the business model. It then faces the decision to pivot (change the business or business model to match the market) or persevere (on the assumption that the core hypothesis for the business is still true).

Pivot or Persevere, Enterprise Style: Many corporate teams and their leaders refuse to acknowledge failure. It's understandable why they do this. In most companies, the reward system is designed in such a way that admitting failure costs money, while denying failure can work to your financial advantage. Although that may be a decent individual strategy, it does not help a big firm learn to innovate. Corporate teams need to redefine success as learning faster, failing early, and minimizing or delaying investment. By applying elements of venture capital funding to corporate ventures, teams can also begin to adopt more agile mindsets. The ability to pivot depends on the corporate VC board's being open to entirely new directions that might be out of the scope of the original charter. Traditional corporate life doesn't prepare you for this process. Lean demands it.

Examples: IBM was a computer company for most of its history, first with mainframes and then with servers and PCs. But as the world changed and its business stagnated, the company pivoted into a global services organization that's been growing ever since. In a different example from P&G, when it developed Nyquil as a cold/flu remedy, initial testing showed that the formulation caused users to feel sleepy. So instead of reformulating, it repositioned Nyquil as the first nighttime cold/flu remedy to help you sleep—and the rest is history.

Innovation Accounting: Risky new ventures require discipline, unlike the "seat-of-the-pants" stereotype promoted about entrepreneurs. Successful entrepreneurs live and breathe metrics; they set goals and growth objectives that are measured frequently and used to adjust direction with agility. Because of these differences in process, the accounting for new ventures must be managed differently. Discovery-driven planning focuses not on accounting in terms of only final output but on measuring what has been learned to support agility.

Innovation Accounting, Enterprise Style: Discovery-driven planning is antithetical to many corporate financial and management teams. It sounds like a bunch of words that can't possibly go together, but it's critical, given that we are measuring an unknown. To follow the lean startup process, there has to be room for discovery along the way. Teams must develop and gain senior team buy-in for milestone-based "learning metrics." This allows for the discovery process to take place while still providing management with confidence that ventures are moving toward viability and success.

Example: At both Intuit and LexisNexis, leaders such as Susan Harman are encouraging the organization to focus on learning metrics and not traditional ROI measures for transformative or whitespace opportunities. "Love metrics" such as net promoter scores provide a simple mechanism for assessing whether the consumer propositions being tested are resonating with consumers and trending in the right direction. The net promoter score (developed by Satmetrix) is a simple 0–10 scale, and only promoters (9–10) are considered successful, as they'll be loyal enthusiasts who will keep buying and actively refer others.

GE DOUBLING DOWN ON LEAN

GE CMO Beth Comstock is embracing lean concepts to help GE move faster and innovate smarter. Partnering with Eric Ries, the company has adapted lean principles in its business model, in a program called FastWorks. The initiative is rolling out to all of GE's six business units, and if past experience is any indication (e.g., Work-Out, Six Sigma), when GE gets behind a new idea, it does so in a big way.

As part of the model, GE has initiated venture capital–type review boards (Growth Boards) that review and approve projects. FastWorks is about helping GE to scale the concepts of speed, agility, and customer engagement and instilling more of an entrepreneurial mindset among these teams. It's a tangible way that GE is trying to encourage its employees to experiment and try new things. Or in the words of Beth Comstock in a recent article: "Fail fast, fail small."

WHEN TO APPLY LEAN STARTUP PRINCIPLES

A lean startup process, while beneficial to a company, is not appropriate in all corporate settings. This is where big companies often lose their way. Convinced that lean tactics are the answer, executives seek to apply them wholesale from the books. In contrast, when we adapt these concepts for corporate clients, we include advice as to when and where they work best.

Ricardo dos Santos, who was previously senior director of new business development for Qualcomm, understands lean in the corporate environment. He is a big proponent of lean methods (like me, he came from the auto industry), and his model (Fig. 2.1) summarizes where the best fit lies for the application of lean startup principles in large companies.

WHEN TO APPLY LEAN

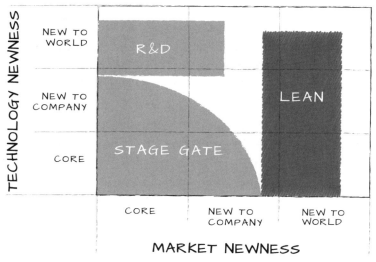

Attribution: Ricardo dos Santos

FIG. 2.1

For core technologies and core markets, stage-gate and traditional product development approaches have been proven and optimized to help companies develop new products and services efficiently. When we start to explore further-out technologies and solutions, that's where advanced R&D efforts come in.

A startup is, in many ways, a search for a business model. So, in a corporate setting, when ventures include business model innovation, lean methods really start to come into their own. The iterative experimentation models can help us quickly build, test, and learn as we explore these opportunities in an environment of high unknowns and attempt to find that winning business model.

BRINGING LEAN TO COCA-COLA

Carie Davis shared with me how she's leading an effort to bring this type of lean thinking into Coca-Cola. The Coca-Cola Company knows that it needs to attack growth and transformative innovation from multiple perspectives. In addition to Davis's group's efforts to internalize entrepreneurial thinking, Coca-Cola has other groups, including a business accelerator program (discussed in chapter 8), a marketing ventures group that connects with digital startups, and a venturing and emerging brands (VEB) group that's searching for the next billion-dollar beverage brand.

CARIE DAVIS,
GLOBAL DIRECTOR, INNOVATION AND ENTREPRENEURSHIP, THE COCA-COLA COMPANY

Carie Davis is championing lean startup and entrepreneurial thinking within Coca-Cola. She's helping to transform the culture and create the company's next generation of entrepreneurial leaders.

I'm in a group at Coca-Cola called "innovation and entrepreneurship." It was started a couple of years ago. The impetus was, essentially, there's disruption happening. Are we able to move into new areas fast enough? Can we recognize new opportunities when they come up? Many times, these opportunities initially look like nothing at all with no real market potential. How can we better cultivate the weeds that might seem like a distraction but could become the next big thing?

We started by building the methods and structure to create internal startups—business model innovation, using our assets in new ways that are adjacent to our core business. That included hiring cofounders with experience using lean startup methods to explore emerging opportunities. Then, when you find product and market fit, do you spin them out? Do you roll them into business units? Do you create new business units? It all depends on what the idea is.

Then leadership said, it's great that you have learned how startups work, witnessed by the people we'd hired and the methods they were using to develop their ideas. What if we were able to give other people in the company those types of skills as well? What would this look like for the people who are working on the core business?

That's what I started to work on. Trying to affect the way people work, changing the culture, can be daunting. In the spirit of working entrepreneurially, we started small. The first thing that we did was to take our own medicine and say, let's run some experiments: can people learn how to work more entrepreneurially, and then can they even apply it inside the walls of a large organization?

We partnered with Startup Weekend; they essentially were doing the same thing in communities. Their objective is to get people excited about starting something. We wanted to give our employees these skills and expose them to these methods from entrepreneurs.

When we did our first internal Startup Weekend at Coca-Cola, we had about 100 people. We just put the word out. It wasn't top down; it was grassroots. We found the people who instantly connected with the message of maybe you have ideas and you don't really know where to start. Maybe you've heard of Startup Weekend and you want to learn more about it. Come and experience this event where you can actually pitch your own idea, form a team, and build something.

The things that came out of it were "I never realized what I could actually accomplish in that amount of time. I could build something in two and a half days." The focus on customer development over product development—essential for entrepreneurs who want to succeed—also resonated with people who went through the experience. It's a fundamental shift in how we approach projects and made a lot of people rethink their product ideas so that we can be sure we're making things people want and need. It really impacted a lot of people who've incorporated these methods into their day jobs. These emerging leaders of the company have now engaged with our group deeply and have new ideas. They want to help us create a movement, and they're actually coming up with new ways that we can continue to do this type of work.

We've done a few other things like failure conferences, to get people used to the idea of calculated risk taking and learning from failure, and hackathons, where we're getting people used to building things instead of just brainstorming. We're giving people the tools to go and make something—to implement it and take initiative. We don't want a culture where you get told what to do. Instead: You have an idea? Go build something.

Carie Davis is a global director of innovation and entrepreneurship for the Coca-Cola Company, where she is a resource to startup ecosystems and builds entrepreneurship within the company. As an experienced industrial designer, she also brings design thinking to these challenges.

BIG COMPANIES ARE NOT STARTUPS

We're touching on lean startup concepts in this chapter, in part because many of the elements of rapid iteration and experimentation are core to the collective disruption framework we'll address in more detail in part 2 of this book.

I'd also recommend these great books about lean startup principles, including more recent work on application in corporate settings.

- *The Lean Startup* by Eric Ries, Crown Business, 2011

- *The Startup Owner's Manual* by Steve Blank and Bob Dorf, K&S Ranch, March 2012

- *Running Lean: Iterate from Plan A to a Plan That Works* by Ash Maurya, O'Reilly Media, March 2012

- *The Lean Enterprise* by Trevor Owens and Obie Fernandez, Wiley, March 2014

Big companies are not startups. They can learn and adapt entrepreneurial mindsets and some methods. But I'm not telling you to try to become a startup. Large companies do many things better than startups, and we don't want to lose sight of these strengths as we pursue transformative innovation. Large companies' ability to bring business discipline, market focus, and scale is a competency that startups can't duplicate. Startups can be chaotic, and some of them focus too much on technology development and not enough on the market and on strategic goals. We want to harness the best of both worlds in creating new sources of growth.

Large and innovative are not mutually exclusive. Apple, Amazon, Medtronic, and Google are just a few examples of large organizations that began their lives as disruptors and have managed to mature into companies that innovate across all three horizons. As you'll hear in later chapters, co-creating with entrepreneurs and startups has been one of their key secrets to success. Adapting lean methods and other entrepreneurial approaches is a way to help you get better at approaching high-risk, high-unknown opportunities outside of your core sustaining innovation efforts. With the help of this new mindset and new set of skills, you can more effectively work with those entrepreneurs who can be important partners in your transformative efforts.

Big companies *can* innovate if they're willing to embrace the changes that entrepreneurialism has brought to the marketplace of ideas.

3

THE EVOLUTION OF OPEN INNOVATION

Popular myth: Steve Jobs was the lone visionary and Apple the lone company behind the iPod.

Reality: Steve Jobs *was* a visionary. But he was not the visionary behind the iPod.

The person who created the concept for the iPod was an independent contractor named Tony Fadell. He had created a breakthrough MP3 player, and when his venture capital ran out, he took the concept to Apple. He had already shopped his idea around to Philips, Microsoft, and Real, who all turned him down. When he brought it to Apple and Steve Jobs, his timing was impeccable. Apple was actively exploring entering this market with its own concepts, and Fadell's vision and direction became the foundation for the first iPod. Apple hired him to lead the team that ultimately created the product that changed everything for Apple—and the world. Fadell eventually left Apple and founded Nest, which he then sold only three years later to Google for $3.2 billion. So while he's far from obscure today, few back in the days of the original iPod had heard of him or understood who was really behind the new device.

Apple isn't usually held up as a prime example of openness, since its secretive development process and proprietary ecosystem seem to run counter to the concept of open collaboration. Yet, in the case of the iPod, Apple leveraged technology and support from at least eight external partners (Toshiba, Synaptics, and TI, to name a few), each which brought critical technology and capabilities. With these partners, Apple developed the iPod in an amazing time frame of fewer than eight months.

Fadell's story helps us see the lesson in this chapter: not all the best ideas will come from inside your walls. Leaders are moving from the system of closed innovation into new, more sophisticated models of external collaboration and co-creation.

"Open innovation" is a term used to describe an environment that ignores the old walls of traditional corporate structure. It suggests that companies should look both internally and externally for ideas and work with partners in sharing both the risk and the reward of innovation. It's a concept most heartily embraced by the technology community and has been championed by Henry Chesbrough in his seminal book, *Open Innovation*.

While in the old days a company on an invention project might be inclined to close ranks and keep secrets, today everyone realizes that no one firm has managed to corner the market on smart people. Reaching out to connect with the best possible talent has become much more acceptable.

As Chesbrough evangelized, open innovation was most influential in the technology world. Today, it's fair to say that the majority of intellectual property (I/P) and technology developments take place in an open innovation environment. While some companies still closely guard their innovation operations, many others are willing to engage in this type of open outreach to make connections, forge alliances, and share the risk and reward of bringing a new product to market.

LEVELING THE PLAYING FIELD

I believe that open innovation isn't really about technology. It's about people. So it made sense to me to create a process for "innovation speed dating." This method can quickly build new relationships, and it puts large companies and entrepreneurs on equal footing. It levels the playing field.

Here's a case in point. In my consulting firm, we were working with a startup led by an entrepreneur named John. He had developed a hand-held semidurable device (good for several months of use before disposal) to provide muscle pain relief using low-intensity transcutaneous electrical nerve stimulation (TENS). He'd been trying to gain interest from companies for several years with no luck. We brought GlaxoSmithKline, Procter & Gamble, Kimberly Clark, Jarden, and other leading companies to meet him and a group of other entrepreneurs at an innovation speed-dating event focused on consumer health monitoring solutions.

At the event, one of these company executives literally pulled out a checkbook and offered John $100,000 on the spot to stop talking to the other companies. John didn't take it. In the following days, he did end up moving into a standstill agreement with one of these firms. Jarden commercialized another technology at the event, a feminine incontinence device called Myself, and the speed-dating format helped both entrepreneurs behind these technologies to leverage the "use it or lose it" principle: create a more competitive environment and change the dynamic for how these corporates dealt with these entrepreneurs. Companies are learning quickly that they need these entrepreneurs as much as the entrepreneurs need them.

Many large companies in industries ranging from CPG and food to pharma, health, and digital technology created dedicated open innovation groups to formalize these external engagement practices during the period from 2003 to around 2010 or 2011. An amazing ecosystem of technology platforms and intermediaries emerged to support these efforts.

I know because I built my initial consulting practice around this movement and lived through its growth and initial maturity. Later, I became a venture capitalist, and my firm Spencer Trask was a pioneering investment group that delivered seed funding for InnoCentive, inno360, and other open innovation platforms that are the leaders in the market today. I've seen the power of open innovation from multiple perspectives, as well as the challenge in scaling open innovation as a core business practice.

A CRISIS OF FAITH

Even with some high-profile case histories from P&G, Unilever, General Mills, and others, many companies trying to embrace the open innovation mindset are finding the time line challenging. It's actually still pretty difficult to find large-scale and compelling data on objective business results across companies from open innovation.

The marketplace is littered with test projects floated by big firms— efforts to partner with the bright minds of entrepreneurs that just never took off and flew like everyone hoped. These are the stories that have led many to lose faith in the open innovation trend. With limited measureable success and companies failing to see a direct payback from their open innovation efforts, the grumbling has begun. A low-level murmur in these communities says it's a fad. Open innovation, the new definition of innovation, its tie to new business creation—they're all fads. If we just hunker down and hold on long enough, things will go back to the way they used to be.

This is a false and dangerous mindset. Waiting for the world to spin backward and take us back to the old days is never a good strategy. Instead, what companies need to do is see the shift in innovation not as a quick fix to what ails them but as a long-term evolution in the business world.

I think those in the business world perceive that the open innovation movement has not (yet) fulfilled its promise, despite more than a decade of concentrated effort, for at least two major reasons. First, we're in the midst of an evolutionary cycle, and open innovation is quietly becoming a more natural and integrated part of doing business. Dedicated and centralized open innovation groups are being reintegrated into the business units where they belong, and the skill set is becoming part of the job description for engineers, product developers, and even marketing managers. This is partly because of the open innovation and crowdsourcing ecosystem that has emerged and is enabling desktop access to expertise, intermediation, and support for corporate managers. So maybe we're being too hard on ourselves about open innovation's performance or prospects.

Second, open innovation programs have been too focused on transactional approaches and incremental core business efforts. Corporate R&D teams are writing scouting briefs, posting them to their websites and to the same online marketplaces, and asking for next-generation packaging, ingredients, or form factors. Where's the long-term competitive advantage in that? It's much easier to look for solutions for near-term to midterm core business problems and insert them into our product/service development processes than it is to develop deeper and earlier-stage collaborations with startups and entrepreneurs who might be the same ones to disrupt your business from the outside.

FROM TRANSACTIONS TO RELATIONSHIPS

Open innovation does not need to backtrack. It needs to expand. This is where my thinking picks up and moves on from the original open innovation discussion. If you are an executive responsible for developing new sources of growth, imagine having the capability to create and engage a network within the broader innovation ecosystem that can not only feed the pipeline but also help you see what's coming next and help you incubate and prove out emerging business opportunities faster and at reduced risk.

John Seely Brown, with Deloitte's Center for the Edge and previously chief scientist at Xerox's famous Palo Alto Research Center (PARC), said it best when he stated, "For open innovation to realize its full potential, it will have to navigate from a narrow focus on transactions to provide much richer support with long-term, trust-based relationships around joint initiatives to address real problems or opportunities."

I've long been a proponent of refocusing open innovation away from a discussion of technologies to a discussion of relationships. In the very near future, if not today, competitive advantage will come not from who has the best technologies but who has the best relationships.

A DECLARATION OF INTERDEPENDENCE

Moving beyond initial transactional approaches and two-party co-development into this more mature state, we'll see relationship-based collaborative networks and, ultimately, innovation ecosystems—truly interdependent organizations. Deeper collaboration and interdependency will be key to success in this new world. "Interdependence" is a great word for this. Just like ecosystems, groups involved in collaborative innovation really do need each other. As a large company, you need the little guys as much as they need you.

Here's a quick story that I originally heard on National Public Radio that illustrates the point of being interdependent.

In the savannas of Africa, elephants and tiny ants have been fighting a long-running battle over little African trees. These elephants eat the trees, and I don't mean nibble. They literally eat the leaves, the limbs—everything until there's nothing left.

So nature hired some ants to protect the trees. These ants are attracted to some tasty sap that the trees make.

Now, when elephants nibble at the trees, no problem. But when they attack the trees and go too far, the ants release a nasty smell, and they swarm all over the elephants. Imagine thousands of ants crawling right up the sensitive trunks of these elephants. It's not pleasant!

Well, this might sound a little counterintuitive, but the ants and the elephants actually need each other. Here's the proof. Scientists did an experiment to see what would happen to the ant-tree alliance if the elephants disappeared. They fenced off an area so that no elephants could get to those trees.

Guess what happened? After a few years, the trees actually died off. Why? Because when they were no longer threatened, the trees stopped producing the sap, and that drove off the guard ants, which were then replaced by other insects that attacked the trees, filled them with holes, and killed them. Nature protected all the species involved by creating a state of interdependence.

Now, from ants and elephants back to business. I used to work at Ford, and I continue to root for the company because in spite of recent resurgence, the domestic auto industry in particular and the auto industry in general continue to struggle. Ford has consolidated its supply base and has put tremendous pressure on its suppliers. It has dictated major cost reductions again and again. So Ford's 2014 performance to date was up from the depths of the recession, but is this happening on the backs of suppliers and mortgaging the company's future in the process? Time will tell. Certainly, Ford is in a brutally competitive market. Many of its major suppliers are struggling, with some at the brink of bankruptcy and others already there. Is Ford throwing in with the ecosystem partners or focusing on a narrow definition of success?

Contrast this with Tesla Motors, where Elon Musk's visionary approach to a performance-based electric vehicle has resulted in the Model S, which *Consumer Reports* recently rated 99 out 100, the highest score the publication has ever given to a vehicle. In addition, in separate tests by the National Highway Safety Administration (NHTSA), the Tesla S received five stars in all categories, a rating that goes to only 1% of the vehicles it tests. When NHTSA tested the roof crush, the testing machine broke before the Tesla's roof would fail.

Tesla's entire business model is built on interdependency, something that's much more the norm in Silicon Valley than on Madison Avenue. Musk even announced in June of 2014 that Tesla was opening up its patents and allowing anyone to use its electric vehicle I/P without fear of being sued. He isn't being altruistic; he simply understands that the advancement of electric vehicle technology helps the entire industry move forward. Tesla's success depends on a growing and dynamic electric vehicle market. In his letter announcing this dramatic move, he said that

Tesla's competitive advantage need not be defensive and that Tesla would compete and win on the merits of its talented engineers.

When you reach that level of maturity in open innovation, the world opens up for you. You can do things you've always dreamed of—maybe even new things you never dreamed possible.

INNOVATION NETWORKS COME IN MANY SHAPES

Building relationship-based networks of innovators and partners can take many forms. I'll address a few common examples of the many types of networks for innovation and collaboration involving large companies and their partners.

Feeder Networks: Think of this type of network as the "exclusive club" model. If your company is large or multinational, thinking of networks within your company as part of a central network is an easy place to start. Feeder networks are developed by proactively identifying the innovators and partners who can bring technology and capabilities to your company. Yes, feeder networks include suppliers, but only a select number, and they include others that aren't suppliers but that are willing to align themselves (even informally) with your company to explore innovation opportunities. Feeder networks are named so because not only are they feeding you early access to what they are working on but also they often are willing to adjust their own development pipelines to more align with your strategic goals if they see enough upside. Identifying and recruiting the right partners that align with your needs is key.

In 2011, Unilever began its award-winning "Partner to Win" program, focused on building deeper relationships with select key suppliers for mutual growth. The company understands that these recurring relationships with partners are underdeveloped assets and that each collaborative program with a partner is faster and more lucrative than the previous one. Unilever has even gone to the point of developing joint business development plans with these partners to lay out a clear framework for collaboration to speed up the process and ensure a longer-term focus.

Internal Networks: In today's global economy, many organizations locate across divisions, time zones, and countries but are united under one corporate banner. Don't overlook the opportunity for intracompany networking (across divisions, brands, or silos).

David Ritter, a director at the Boston Consulting Group (and former CTO at InnoCentive), talks about how internal collaboration is a necessary precursor to successful external collaboration. He's shared the story of Syngenta (a major agriculture science company) and the power of its internal collaboration systems that are treated like an internal open innovation network. Problems are posed to these networks, and according to Ritter, they are able to find at least partial solutions 70% of the time, before even reaching out to the broader external sources of technology and innovation. Ritter notes that these results are typical for companies that take a structured approach and carefully formulate the problems before posting and facilitating the process from end to end. Less structured enterprise networks don't tend to yield high solution rates.

Cisco is a client of mine, and so I've seen firsthand how the company has developed a strong capability for collaboration within and across business units. You'd expect a company that builds and sells collaboration tools such as WebEx to know a thing or two about internal collaboration, and it does. Cisco has invested heavily in applying enterprise collaboration tools across the business and claims a 900% return on investment to date. Through its I-Zone, any of Cisco's 60,000 employees can propose a business idea, work collaboratively with other employees to refine it, and, if accepted, be part of launching a new business.

Peer-to-peer Networks: These types of networks involve noncompetitive, or even competitive, companies sharing insights and co-developing opportunities. While standards-based industry consortia probably fit this model, I'm referring more to commercially driven collaborative efforts.

As an example, I was involved in founding and managing a peer-to-peer network for mobile innovation called Third Screen Marketplace. Starting in 2009, we brought together a group of leading CPG, food, and consumer health brands that understood the huge emerging opportunity for brand building on mobile. I'll talk more about this network in chapter 6 in the context of discovery. The initiative was far from easy, but it clearly demonstrated the power of collaboration to accelerate adoption and aggregation of opportunities through a networked model.

Events and Forums: Events and forums are, in many ways, the mechanism to actualize many of the networks above. But they are also a way to experiment with a network before committing to it on a longer-term basis. Think of these types of networks as innovation crowdsourcing—by invitation: discrete events aimed at creating and, eventually, nurturing a network of innovators.

In my consulting work, our team helped GSK expand its collaboration with a leading university via a series of summits where new connections and opportunities could be surfaced and explored. We first conducted research and interviews on both sides to better understand needs, capabilities, and priorities. We used this information to structure large-scale summits where GSK shared its needs more deeply, and this university highlighted areas of research aligned with GSK's needs. The forums included both group sessions and one-on-one sessions where deeper relationships could be built. Several promising new development projects emerged directly from these connections. After the success of this initiative, the relationship between GSK and this university flourished.

All of these approaches (and many others) are relevant to building networks and getting plugged into the larger innovation ecosystem.

The problem today is that many companies doing open innovation have the view that they are at the center of the ecosystem. If you are a Unilever or a P&G, you can probably do that, and I wouldn't argue against the need for that. My company is helping some of these larger companies build their own networks, but I believe that you need to plug into the larger ecosystem as well. I actually see a web of relationships in which you have your own network where you're at the center but you're also part of the larger ecosystems where you are grouped with others—peers and potential competitors—in the flow of ideas and not necessarily owning all of those relationships.

BUILDING YOUR INNOVATION NETWORK

We've discussed various types of networks and the benefits they can provide. An innovation network doesn't spring up fully formed in an existing company. This section is aimed at providing some of the basic considerations in building and supporting networks in alignment with your innovation and growth goals.

In the end, it's not a linear prescriptive process. Networks should be nurtured and not managed from a mindset of control. I recall a specific project I worked on where a client company asked my firm to help it build a network in a market where it was somewhat of a newcomer. We were able to get this client engaged with other leading companies in the space through a peer-to-peer network. It was all working very well until a few companies in this new collaboration began to undertake some projects between themselves that had sprung out of introductions that our network events had initiated. To me, this was a very good and healthy sign of interest and collaboration. To my client, it was a sign of losing control and a feeling that since the company had invested time and money in jumpstarting the effort, it somehow had the right to be involved in every collaboration that might emerge. Its controlling behavior eventually undermined the effort, and the formal network was abandoned. Networks need to be nurtured and developed, but trying to control them in a command-and-control style will never work. That said, you can take some practical steps to move beyond ad hoc approaches to building and engaging with networks more productively.

Set Clear Goals: The process starts with determining what goals you hope to achieve with your innovation network.

Every company has a growth strategy. Growth can come from new geographies, markets, channels, and technologies. From that growth opportunity, you need a network strategy that defines the path and incorporates recognition of the company's competencies. The specific strategies should be aimed at whatever you determine are marketplace opportunities and gaps, either underserved segments or underserved needs.

For example, if you are a consumer-based company, you might want to create new connections and partnerships in the professional channel of your market. This would be a different strategy and approach than, say, identifying emerging technologies in key areas of interest for incorporation into your product development.

Open innovation networks can support your efforts in everything from scanning and trend tracking to solving specific technical challenges and finding partners for specific co-development activities. Thinking about the role you want your network to play will help in defining the charter for creating it.

Identify Key Players: Your sources of ideas and individuals or companies for your network depend on your specific situation, your industry, and your strategic goals but use both strategic goals and technology goals to identify these crucial sources. Network members may cut across technology and market expertise, but you should begin by looking at influential and respected players in the technology arena or market space. Just as in creating any high-performance team, I find it important to identify and recruit a few influential and highly respected members both for the content they bring and for their ability to help you grow and further develop the network. Early players will likely help to identify additional sources of ideas and information that may not be obvious to you.

Next, map your network and key players in the technology and marketing space. Draw the interconnections you know about. Add the new sources and players to your map. Look at gaps and develop strategies to build the missing connections. In an upcoming example of the Weight Management Collaborative, further described below, we actually mapped more than 150 leading players across food, devices, services, apparel, technology, and other categories in our initial planning of this peer-to-peer network.

Informally Launch: Informal event launching allows participants to create early relationships. This is a time for the sharing of organic best practices and the development of one-to-one relationships. For example, a company can conduct special events and forums to test interest and fit; this is also a good way to weed out those who are not really committed to further involvement. Informal approaches also let everyone test the waters. Participants can check out potential partners without the difficulty of having to uninvite them if they're not a fit.

Finally, you're more likely to get some early involvement if partners don't need to initially make a long-term commitment. After some discussion of valuable connections and opportunities, everyone will see where there are mutual fits. Over time, the informal events can migrate and evolve into a more formal network.

Keep it low key and let the right relationships develop over time. The network will emerge and evolve. Don't force it too quickly or too formally. And don't get stuck in your views of what the network should look like. I'd take passionate involvement over perfect partners that fit my preconceived notions any time.

Formalize and Expand the Network: To move beyond ad hoc efforts and accelerate open innovation, the network needs to be developed and nurtured. In order to make that happen, create more formal mechanisms for network operation such as forums for ongoing communication. Strive to create a sense of community. Now is a good time to introduce enabling technologies such as social networks, collaboration software, and online portals. Even as that happens, don't forget to include face-to-face meetings. This is still really all about relationships.

At this state, you can start exploratory collaboration projects such as joint research and technology development explorations.

Experiment and Evolve: Now let's talk about nurturing a network's evolution, specifically, about using experiments and initiatives to strive for innovation and business outcomes. As the network develops and matures, you need to create specific initiatives, projects, and co-development efforts as catalysts. Innovation is complex; collaborative innovation is more complex. It's not linear but fluid. You can't predict when a consumer need will be uncovered, or when an enabling technology will emerge, or when a marketplace opportunity will present itself. That's why you need to create mechanisms and approaches that help you continually look for the intersections of these three areas.

A FEEDER NETWORK IN PRACTICE

Ed Kaczmarek, at the time the director of innovation and emerging technology for Mondelēz International (previously Kraft's snack business), was charged with connecting and collaborating with emerging digital technology startups to support Mondelēz brands, including icons such as Oreo, Nabisco, Honey Maid, Cadbury, and many others. Kaczmarek, along with Bonin Bough (VP of global media), created and executed a very interesting model for Mondelēz that helped to attract innovative mobile-centric marketing solutions for its brands in three areas: mobile at retail, social TV, and location-aware technologies.

Kaczmarek and Bough were forward thinking in treating this as a broader network opportunity and actively engaged agencies, VCs, complementary brands, and other ecosystem enablers, a strategy that also gave the initiative more critical mass to attract the best digital and mobile innovators.

ED KACZMAREK,
COFOUNDER OF THE BRAND ACCELERATOR (PREVIOUSLY DIRECTOR OF INNOVATION AND EMERGING TECHNOLOGY, MONDELĒZ INTERNATIONAL)

Ed Kaczmarek explains how Mobile Futures helped Mondelēz International develop competitive advantage by partnering with startups, the way it drove a cultural transformation in the company, and how the network Mondelēz built helped make it happen.

When I was at Mondelēz, I was global director of innovation and emerging technology. For a few years, I worked with startups one at a time. I would pay from a central budget, and I would invite brands to work with us on each startup engagement. We did that pretty successfully.

Then we began architecting the Mobile Futures program. We called it "Mobile Futures: The Future in 90 Days" because we felt that we had to put a sense of urgency on it or it would turn into just any other project. Along with Bonin Bough (VP of global media), I had to sell the value to the brands. We were paying for the program at the center, but we were asking the brands to put in money to pay for the actual pilot. The money would go directly to the startups for their different pilot engagements.

We started the program at Kraft Foods before we separated and became Mondelēz International. Within 90 days our goal was to connect eight brands with nine startups, and we actually had eight pilots in market within the 90 days. One of the pilots we had some technology challenges with, so that trailed a little bit.

The primary goals were cultural transformation and to drive competitive advantage by collaborating with startups. It drove this newfound passion for marketers to be creative and to actually feel the art of marketing, not push it off on their agency to do. It had an extraordinary snowball effect within the company. I had product scientists e-mailing me saying that they were proud to be part of a company that believed in a program like Mobile Futures.

We started by defining the marketing challenges and had startups submit into the process, and then we short-listed them. We had two pitch days at the East Hanover offices where the marketers could hear the start-ups' pitch and choose whom they wanted to work with. Next we had the marketers go on an immersion week. They lived with the startups at their location for one week. Many of the startups also came and spent one or two days with the marketers at the Mondelēz offices. That really started the whole cultural transformation—being a part of the startup team. One of our marketers said to me, "We did creative briefs in two hours with all of us sitting at a table. Why does it take my agency two months to do a creative brief?"

Because we were creating Mobile Futures where nothing like that had existed before, we put together the Mobile Futures Network of Partners not only to give us some fire power to get the startups interested in the company but also to learn from all of them. For instance, we had Viacom and AT&T as part of it. This was not only to learn but also to leverage their brand power. The VCs and other partners in our Mobile Futures network are there to guide us. If I have question on something, I at least have someone who's knowledgeable in that area who can answer it.

It was working. People were happy; then, more people wanted to be involved in it, and they trusted it a little bit more. Since that time, the company has created a global program and expanded it.

In my new role with Brand Accelerator, we have our process of starting with the marketing challenges and working to solve them with startups. Now I can bring my experience to other big brands and also bring the ability to nurture teams through the process.

Something else we learned at Mobile Futures was that brands need to work with startups that already have a viable product; once a pilot is completed, they need to be able to scale with the brand. There's nothing more frustrating: a brand loves a pilot and is excited about the results, and then the startup says, "I need another eight months before I can scale." You can understand why the brand would be disappointed. You don't want to hear "What did I just waste my time on? Why did I do this? Now I want to do it bigger, and they can't do it."

In talking with other brands, I've had so many people come up to me and say, "I know we should be doing this, but we have no idea where to begin." We didn't know where to begin, either, but you just have to dive in. Of course, we had the experience of working with startups for a couple of years. It was a matter of not only teaching our marketers how to do it but also showing where it could ultimately help them solve marketing challenges.

_____

Ed Kaczmarek is cofounder and managing director of Brand Accelerator, which helps leading brand companies develop competency in partnering with startups to ignite entrepreneurship. In his role with Mondelēz International, Kaczmarek led efforts to work with digital startups, including the highly successful Mobile Futures initiative.

A PEER-TO-PEER NETWORK IN PRACTICE

A few years ago, I led the creation of a commercially driven program called the Weight Management Collaborative. It included leading brands as well as a highly vetted group of subject matter experts and technology providers focused on consumer weight management. The premise was that consumers would benefit from new solutions that were better integrated across products, services, online support, and other areas.

In creating the initiative, we first mapped the ecosystem across everything from food, to devices, to behavioral support. While each of these companies had a role in improving consumers' health and weight management in particular, these same companies were missing opportunities for collaborative approaches that could create new value for the consumer and new business opportunities for the companies themselves.

We identified a short list of complementary players who we believed could provide valuable support and were leaders and innovators in their categories. In this case, we began through a series of no-obligation summits with representatives from these companies, and this provided our client (and its potential partners) the opportunity to "try on" the relationships and to explore in a low-pressure environment whether opportunities for collaboration really existed.

Well, they did. As expected, some of the early invitees were not invited back, and some chose to opt out, but those that remained then began a series of highly fruitful consumer-focused projects and teaming agreements for new commercial opportunities—ones that these individual companies could not have addressed alone. Joint development projects emerged among various groups of two or three key players that were progressed through consumer studies and in-market pilots to quickly assess consumer and market interest. These cross-company initiatives likely never would have been possible without the network and ability to quickly learn from the market together before proceeding to deeper, more traditional collaboration.

The collaborative took only three months from initiation and mapping key players to holding the first summits. It took only six to eight months from initiation for highly fruitful joint development programs to emerge. How long would it take in a traditional approach to reach out to complementary players, find areas of common interest, and put the mechanisms and agreements in place to explore them?

SOME DO'S AND DON'TS FOR INNOVATION NETWORKS

Do:

- Align strategic objectives and acknowledge differing goals

- Ensure senior management support from core network members

- Treat all partners with respect; avoid large company centric

- Focus on learning, not just results

- Create a sense of community; simplify communication

Don't:

- Overly structure the network

- Manage as a hierarchy

- Allow conflicts to fester without being addressed

- Forget I/P ownership discussions and guidelines

- Keep networks in place after they have served their purpose

You usually think of ecosystems in nature as the big guys eating the small guys. But in ecosystems—interdependent ecosystems—as in business, it's not the big that eat the small; it's the fast that eat the slow. Be fast. Learn to collaborate with a network of fast entrepreneurial partners. Remember that future competitive advantage will be measured not by who has the best technologies but by who has the best relationships.

PART 2:

COLLABORATE TO DISRUPT

4

EMBRACING COLLECTIVE DISRUPTION

In the first part of this book, I've told you that the game has changed and that engaging with innovation ecosystems is important. This second part is a primer on how to play the new game, including how to engage and leverage innovation ecosystems to support transformative innovation and new business creation. In this chapter, I'll summarize the manifesto for collective disruption and set the stage for more specific frameworks and approaches to be shared in upcoming chapters.

I've extensively discussed the impact of speed on corporate innovation. If the company of yesteryear could get by pumping out a new product or service on a yearly or biyearly schedule, those days are through. We live and work today in what author James Gleick called "the epoch of the nanosecond." The concept of innovation has to evolve. What's needed is more than injecting speed into the existing innovation process. We need to embrace new structures and networked approaches, combined with the best of approaches that innovators through history such as da Vinci, Edison, and Jobs have demonstrated.

The dynamic nature of business today means that not only innovation but also business needs to be redefined. I was taught in business school that a company should seek a sustainable competitive advantage—a manageable, long-term, and predictable existence; now, a company needs a new construct. The evolution demands new definitions of success. It needs what author Rita McGrath called "transient competitive advantage." Because these advantages are transient, the company needs them over and over and over.

In this way, we see that companies need more than a speed injection. Innovation must be redefined, and, along with it, the business must be redefined. Companies need to find a sustainable way to continually reinvent themselves. They need an existence in which they can milk the current business and all the while create a series of new businesses that build on the last but create a new growth curve. Companies must learn to play the disruption game. This is not easy because a company can't disrupt itself—at least not without help.

Generally speaking, disruption in the business world is something that comes from outside the walls and is decidedly unwelcome. But what if that disruption could be made part of the corporate family? Suppose the outsiders could be embraced in a way that benefited everyone.

COLLECTIVE VALUE CREATION

When I worked at Spencer Trask, an early-stage investment firm founded by Kevin Kimberlin, we had developed a unique model that was a hybrid between traditional angel groups and more traditional venture capital firms. Kevin's vision was to amplify our ability to accelerate growth of start-ups by turning our 4,000+ high-net-worth investors into a value creation network. Our ideal investors sought to make a profit for sure, but they also wanted to make a difference. Bringing together entrepreneurs with big ideas and investors, many who were seasoned corporate executives or entrepreneurs, in a unique value creation network is a great model. Beyond investment, this network accelerated growth through director positions and leveraging connections, advice, technical assistance, and numerous other ways. Ciena, InnoCentive, Health Dialog, and Myriad Genetics are just a few of the successful ventures that benefited from this value creation approach.

So why can't corporations and startups partner in venture co-creation in a model similar to that of value creation networks? It's not easy, but it's the future—and that future is unfolding today at leading companies that are learning to collaborate with early-stage entrepreneurs to create not only new products and services but also innovative new business models and new symbiotic ecosystems.

In this and the following chapters, I'll share examples from P&G, Jarden, GE, Coca-Cola, Johnson & Johnson, Lowe's, Cisco, and others who are learning to partner in new ways with entrepreneurs, accelerators, and startups in the entrepreneurial ecosystem to co-create new growth platforms and new businesses.

LEVERAGING POLARITIES

Corporations and startups are often thought of as opposite ends of the spectrum, like oil and water. But remember: opposites attract. Collective disruption is about harnessing the power of two seemingly disparate groups and aligning the best of both worlds at each stage of the value creation process.

Some years back, a personal coach taught me about a personal and organizational development model called polarity thinking (www. PolarityPartnerships.com). The theory, developed by Dr. Barry Johnson, states that through our adult lives, most of us have progressed and succeed through effective "either/or" problem solving. For example, my engineering training instilled in me a thought process of defining the problem, identifying alternatives, and then arriving at the single best solution. But life today is much more complex than that. Many challenges aren't solvable in the traditional sense, and we need to learn to leverage polarities as an ongoing process. In organizational design, a good example is decentralized approaches versus centralized approaches. Each has its advantages and its place, and each has a downside if overfocused as the "solution" to the neglect of the other.

In our context, the apparent paradoxes in corporate and entrepreneurial approaches are polarities that we can harness. Our job as business leaders is to leverage these corporate/entrepreneurial polarities in the context of our work. F. Scott Fitzgerald said, "The test of a first-rate intelligence is the ability to hold two opposing ideas in the mind at the same time and still retain the ability to function."

I've used the Polarity Map to highlight polarities and how we can leverage them in the context of corporates and startups collaborating in transformative innovation and new business creation.

POLARITY MAP FOR COLLECTIVE DISRUPTION

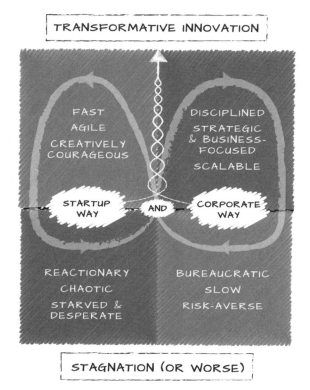

FIG. 4.1

This model (Fig. 4.1) shows two neutral poles at either end of the horizontal axis. Using the metaphor of breathing, you need to both inhale and exhale. Neither is better or more important than the other. In our case, the horizontal axis is made up of the startup way and the corporate way. We need both, and they are interdependent.

The upper sections of the quadrant are the positive results of focusing on each of the respective poles. The positive results of focusing on the corporate way are more disciplined, strategic, and scalable opportunities. The positive results of focusing on the startup way are being fast, agile, and courageous (e.g., smart risk taking).

The lower sections of the quadrant are the negative results of over-focusing on one pole at the expense of the other. The negative results of overfocusing on the startup way are chaos, opportunism, and being starved (of money and resources). The negative results of overfocusing on the corporate way are being slow, bureaucratic, and risk averse.

The box at the top is the higher purpose. It answers the question of "Why invest in leveraging this polarity?" It goes beyond the upside of each pole. In our case, the higher purpose is transformative innovation that is customer and market focused. Similarly, at the bottom is the deeper fear. If we don't invest in managing this polarity, we end up with stagnation or, worse, decline and extinction.

The action steps (Fig. 4.2) are ways that we can leverage the positive elements of each pole. Similarly, early warnings are indicators that we may be overfocusing and getting into the downside of a pole.

POLARITY ACTION STEPS AND EARLY WARNINGS

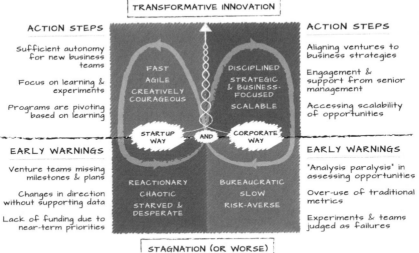

FIG. 4.2

We need both the startup way and the corporate way to succeed at transformational innovation and new business creation. I believe that this is a powerful model for viewing corporate and startup collaboration. Multiple important polarities exist within this larger frame of corporate/entrepreneurial collaboration. Other examples of polarities to leverage include autonomy/integration, risk taking/risk avoidance, and speed/discipline to name just a few.

You'll see in upcoming chapters how we can use the complementary strengths of each of these approaches in a virtuous circle of natural tensions. The collective disruption framework, which is introduced in the next chapter, is designed specifically to maximize the benefits of the interdependencies of these polarities from conception to scale-up and reintegration of new growth opportunities. I hope you find it as useful as I have in thinking about living in these two worlds at the same time.

STRATEGIC FOCUS AND LEADERSHIP SUPPORT

To know whether your company is ready to undertake this path toward collective disruption, start with this question: Is your company strategically focused on the need for transformative innovation or new business creation? To justify the effort, seek strong alignment with corporate strategy. If you find a strategic imperative to develop new growth platforms with more transformative innovation, then you will likely gain support for these efforts when the going gets tough. Remember that these efforts go against the core DNA of most companies, so don't expect an easy ride.

In nearly every case I've studied, senior management support (or lack thereof) seems to be *the* key element that makes or breaks an organization's attempt to develop breakout approaches to creating new sources of growth. In the successful companies we've studied, these transformational organizations or teams report to senior management and seldom to the core business lines. Beware the temptation in the business units to deprioritize these efforts in the face of near-term financial and competitive pressures. The CEO is the leader who can best ensure a balanced portfolio across current core business and future new business efforts.

ORGANIZING AND GOVERNING

The goal in these efforts is to strike the right balance of integration and autonomy. While the question of organizational design has no universal best answer, some of the most effective new business creation groups we've seen (e.g., Jarden, P&G, and Coca-Cola) create dedicated organizations but also put in place mechanisms to encourage alignment with business units both on front-end strategy and on back-end reintegration of these businesses when they're ready to scale. In my opinion, a good metaphor for successful organization design in managing transformative innovation or new business creation is "an island with a bridge to the mainland." I'll revisit this concept in subsequent chapters as we begin to explore the process of collective disruption.

In traditional portfolio management, the emphasis is rightly on significant upfront diligence and planning prior to committing resources or funding for strategic initiatives or major programs. While upfront planning and definition are still important, we need to shift our thinking in the context of transformative innovation.

This is a portfolio of higher-risk opportunities with more unknowns. We generally don't have the data we like to see as corporate executives, and that's where entrepreneurial thinking comes in again. Venture capitalists spread their bets in large part because it's too difficult to pick the winners upfront. So in corporate venturing and new business development activities, we should be looking at a broader set of opportunities and placing smaller bets on each and then running a set of experiments using lean principles to quickly prove or disprove our key hypotheses with minimum time and investment. We need to take on the challenge of rethinking governance processes to allow for early-stage experimentation across a broader range of opportunities. Likewise, we need to be thinking of external partners (startups, suppliers, others) as labs that can experiment cheaply on our behalf.

P&G, Whirlpool, Qualcomm, and others have successfully used a venture capital model in how horizon 3 activities are proposed, selected, and funded. I think it's a good model to consider, but, of course, each company's situation and needs are unique. One other consideration: rather than funding by specific initiative, empower your new business creation teams by funding each strategic focus area. As long as these areas are aligned with the strategic priorities, let the teams divide their spending among individual projects. You'll have faster learning, and you're putting the decision making in the hands of those with the direct knowledge of opportunities. Providing funding via tranches is also a good way to manage financial risk in these setups.

NEW SKILLS AND MINDSETS

A new breed of corporate leader is emerging—one that understands the polarities we discussed in this chapter and can bridge entrepreneurial approaches within a corporate environment. A change in strategy can't happen with just good outside advice. The ability to make the necessary cultural and structural changes over the long term requires an internal champion—someone who makes it his or her life's work to revamp the innovation process in this new way for the betterment of the firm. If it's simply the test project of someone in R&D, it will likely stall and die. Just as internal evangelists promote change from within on issues of sustainability or marketing, the shift to this new kind of innovation needs true, long-term, high-ranking leadership.

I've been inspired by the executives I work with and the many I interviewed for this book who are charged with creating future sources of growth for their companies. They may be general managers; they might reside in R&D or marketing; or, in some cases, they could be leaders over dedicated new business creation organizations. In all cases, the capabilities they are building span a unique skill set.

Companies endeavoring to take this journey should be looking for a different type of leader internally to bridge these two worlds. This unique skill set is what's needed, and the smarter companies are putting in place the types of people who have these skills. You may have some of these people already; often they are the credible, respected innovators on the inside who are leaving to join startups. These people are valuable and difficult to find, so do whatever you can to not lose them. Companies, investors, and entrepreneurs who know how to engage and leverage these ecosystems will be the winners. They can bridge these two worlds because they have empathy, with both:

Corporate empathy:

- Strong business strategy and sense

- High levels of credibility in the organization

- Persistence, inclusiveness, and resiliency

- Open-mindedness, unlikely to succumb to "false negatives"

Entrepreneurial empathy:

- Ability to appreciate entrepreneurs and speak their language

- Creativity, not fitting the traditional corporate mold

- Ability to translate raw ideas into business opportunities and connect dots

- A bias to action and aversion to analysis paralysis

The new environment will call for a new set of "star" players. Individuals who were successful in the old methodology may not be suited to the new demands. Those who never would have been considered hirable by your company may now be just what you need. Perhaps you never before needed an individual who internally championed outside collaboration. You need that bridge champion now.

ENTREPRENEURIAL FROM THE OUTSIDE IN

Beyond the core benefit of co-creating businesses that benefit both corporations and startups, another benefit to corporations is the cultural transformation that can be accelerated by working side by side with entrepreneurs and exposing your teams to their mindsets and approaches. I believe that deep engagement and collaboration with entrepreneurs are important ways to actually begin changing your culture for the better.

Ed Kaczmarek from Mondelēz told me as much in describing Mobile Futures. "It starts the marketers thinking like entrepreneurs, where they can begin breaking down all of the processes that they have known to try to make them better, to be better marketers and do better marketing and engage consumers in new and innovative ways. It very much was cultural transformation that we designed the program to achieve. I think what it also did was it showed all big brands that it's possible and that you have to lead. We're not going to sit around and wait until all of our competitors are doing work with startups. We're going to be the ones out there leading and forging ahead."

I developed the entrepreneurial mindset model (Fig. 4.3) as a useful way to illustrate how many organizations typically approach risky innovations versus how seasoned innovators (including successful entrepreneurs) do. For the typical company, at the beginning of any strategic innovation initiative, everyone's excited and optimistic: we've got a great idea, and we're going to rule the world (the dreaming stage). Then, we may encounter challenges, and we face failure (the doubting stage). The process is never as easy as we think it will be. Failure is a natural and useful element of innovation; it's how we learn and adapt our solutions or determine whether the time has come to try another challenge.

ENTREPRENEURIAL MINDSET MODEL

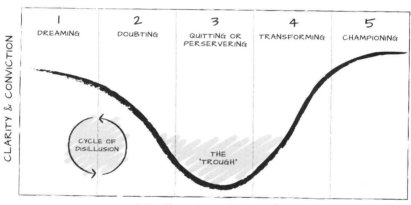

FIG. 4.3

As we develop innovative concepts into real-world practical solutions, we're learning more. The problem isn't as simple, and we begin to truly understand the complexity of the challenge. It's this third stage (quitting or persevering) that truly separates innovators from dreamers. Those who persevere and don't often quit experience a transformation of having worked through the challenges, and, thus, they acquire a new confidence built on deep knowledge and experience.

Those organizations and individuals that never progress beyond the early stages become hardened in their positions and adopt ever more risk-averse approaches to future endeavors. They enter a vicious cycle of disillusion.

Successful entrepreneurs (and visionary corporate innovators) understand the power of this informed clarity. Individuals and organizations that repeatedly fight their way through to transformational outcomes acquire an ability to champion innovative and potentially risky ideas. It's not blind optimism; it's a recognition and calmness about the process of trial and error and a development of informed instinct as to when the time is appropriate to continue with the challenge or move on to the next one. I believe that one of the best (and fastest) ways to evolve an organization's culture to one that supports entrepreneurial mindsets and agility is to work alongside those who have crossed this chasm.

BRIDGING TWO WORLDS

The Brandery is a leading business incubator, based in Cincinnati, Ohio, and I'm a mentor there. It's unique in part because of its marketing and brand heritage, being in the land of Procter & Gamble. The Brandery's model includes close relationships with corporations and leverages the best of the polarities of both the startup way and the corporate way. It is consistently ranked as the top accelerator in terms of mentorship. Startup teams benefit immensely from some of the best brand and marketing experts in the world. I can speak from personal experience when I say that these same mentors (agency and corporate execs) gain great inspiration from the passion and sense of urgency that these startup founders bring to their businesses.

DAVID KNOX,
CMO, ROCKFISH AND COFOUNDER OF THE BRANDERY

We can learn a lot from this ex-P&G marketer who cofounded the Brandery (www.brandery.org), one of the top incubators in the United States. Knox talks about the opportunity for corporate brands to get better tied into the startup ecosystem, not only for ideas but also for talent.

If you look at the history of the Brandery, collaboration with corporations was really there from day one. When we came up with the idea, I was still at P&G. An initial inspiration was seeing how poorly the brand world was really understood, both by startups and by venture capitalists. Many of the startups had business plans that hinged on the dollars that brand marketers had but didn't really have a true understanding of what we (P&G) did. So it was important for us to build that relationship, starting with P&G but then naturally leveraging the alumni network that took people to places like Kellogg's and PepsiCo and other companies across the board.

In our startup recruiting process, we reach out to some of our brand marketing mentors and ask what their business challenges are. What are they looking for in solutions? That helps impact as we think about recruiting for the Brandery startups. When we have an interesting company, we'll often send it through to some of our mentors during the recruitment process and say, "What do you think about this? Does this meet your needs? Would you find this interesting?"

If you look at corporate development and innovation across the board, there's a lot we can learn from the tech community. If you look at Google, they almost seem to encourage their employees to leave Google to go create a startup with the desire to then buy that startup back once they get over the hurdle initially. I think they recognize that in that incubation stage the big company can do more harm than good, so they would rather let you leave and then go buy you back for $10–$20 million.

If you work for a large company and then leave to go do a startup, you're almost blacklisted for two years: "We can't talk to you because you might be unfairly using your previous relationships." I think corporations, especially more on the CPG side, need to be open to buying innovation and being OK with we're going to spend $5, $15, $20 million to buy really interesting small companies for the people and for the product. But that's just not in the DNA of most of them.

There's this myth of the hoodie-wearing, sandal-wearing founder as the best way to have a successful startup. There was an interesting study on the Boston innovation ecosystem. Turns out, a lot of the IPOs over the last five years had been driven by experienced businesspeople and MBAs. If that is true, that's a source of talent for a lot of traditional CPGs. Some of the best talent may be graduating from these MBA programs, and they're deciding to do the startup world instead of doing the traditional path. So for corporations there are real opportunities to acqui-hire versus just promote from within.

My advice to large companies getting started? Be willing to participate in the startup community where you are going that extra mile to help that startup and that investor out. It will pay tremendous dividends because it builds your social currency that you're not just a big-brand person. You get the reputation of being somebody who is really helpful, who pays it forward, who helps people get things done—not somebody who does a bunch of meetings and throws the weight of your big company around.

David Knox worked for Procter & Gamble for nearly a decade as part of the corporate digital team that led P&G to be named to AdAge's Digital A-List. He is a cofounder of the Brandery, recognized as one of the top 10 startup accelerators in the United States. He joined the marketing agency Rockfish (www.rockfishdigital.com) as CMO in 2010 and has been a key leader as the agency tripled in size and was recently acquired by WPP.

COLLECTIVE DISRUPTION AND CORPORATE VENTURING

I'd like to draw a distinction between the collaboration I'm promoting with this approach and the traditional transactional approach of many corporate venture capital arms. Corporate VCs such as GSK's SR One can add significant value for the parent but are usually driven first by creating attractive financial returns and second by providing strategic value to the company's innovation portfolio. Most are corporate versions of the traditional venture capital model, providing funding, some oversight, mentoring, and connections and hopefully betting on the right portfolio of early-stage technology companies. Traditionally, the corporate side and the venturing side have had very little interaction.

In the collective disruption model, while funding may be part of the formula, it's much more about direct collaboration and engagement with entrepreneurs that can enable the transformational portion of the innovation portfolio. Some of the smarter corporate venturing groups I've seen are now blending these models, for example, making early-stage investment in startups that might be helpful to their corporate brethren in entering new markets or channels. Even better, I know a few that are partnering with their business colleagues in new ways and providing the business with an alternative path to incubate big ideas while protecting nascent opportunities from the corporate anti-bodies.

Johnson & Johnson's innovation centers provide a great example of this new model. In four innovation centers (California, Boston, London, Shanghai), J&J is identifying and engaging with early-stage startups and entrepreneurs in mutually beneficial collaboration. While equity investment is common, it's not a requirement. J&J is gaining early access and relationships with a vetted talent base of scientists from academia and startups. The entrepreneurs gain critically important support from J&J scientific, regulatory, and business experts residing in these innovation centers. The initial focus was pharmaceutical development and has since expanded to support its large medical device and consumer products businesses. Says Paul Stoffels, chief scientific officer for Johnson & Johnson, "The objective is to access a diversity of thinking that can be very difficult to get in a large organization. We can tap into work that's going on here in academic and research settings and find the science to solve problems in the shortest possible time." J&J is also directly involved in company formation with entrepreneurs. Through its Entrepreneur Innovator Program, entrepreneurs can bring interesting technology or business ideas to J&J. If J&J sees significant value in the idea, it might assist them in company formation, support business plan development, provide office and incubator space, and provide additional financial and advisory support—all while the entrepreneur retains 100% ownership. Why? Because J&J understands the importance of early engagement and positioning it as the partner of choice.

LET'S CHALLENGE THE DISRUPTION PARADIGM

We've all been accepting of the paradigm that the startups are what always disrupt large, established companies. Through the collective disruption model, large companies can engage and leverage the entrepreneurial ecosystem to create new market-disrupting businesses. It's a new way of organizing a business so that it concurrently runs strong/steady and nimble/disruptive. Collective disruption combines the best of big brands and startup nation.

In the next chapter, I'll provide the overall framework for moving beyond theory and into practice. Subsequent chapters then provide more detailed how-tos for each of the four (iterative) phases of this framework.

5

THE COLLECTIVE
DISRUPTION FRAMEWORK

In this chapter, I'll introduce a framework for collective disruption that will help you move from theory to execution. I've spent time in the early chapters telling you why; now, I'm going to tell you how. You can't just call a company meeting and order everyone to innovate in a new way or else. Companies need a framework, one they can adopt and evolve into what works for them. Framework is a better label than process, because it's not a prescriptive, linear progression. It's a phased approach to engaging with the ecosystem and defining and developing big ideas collaboratively. By its nature of working across organizations, we need to think of it more like guardrails that move us in the right direction but allow for flexibility and iteration along the way.

As I have said, the action in disruptive value creation is happening in startups and emerging technology firms. Large companies know how to market, brand, distribute, scale, and optimize. These same companies need to find ways to leverage the value creators in startups to fuel their growth with entire new businesses. Large companies today have shown interest in learning from lean startups and creating their own "intrapreneuring" programs. While they certainly can learn to be more entrepreneurial, they're missing the bigger point, and they are often mistakenly taking the old corporate-centric view of this new world: one that seeks to take new ideas, bring them inside the walls, and assert ownership. What they really need to do is to engage and nurture external ecosystems of innovators and startups to fuel new business creation activities. It's not the old castle wall approach, that's for sure. But it's the way forward.

Some companies are already making this a reality. In the battle of the picture makers, Fuji is evolving and thriving thanks to its willingness to disrupt and replace its core businesses, while Kodak continues to recede into the sepia-toned background of our old, aging, no longer relevant brands.

What Fujifilm did was recognize that its core business of film was dying. While Kodak moved slowly to diversify incrementally, Fuji was reinventing itself into new categories and working with new outside partners to do so.

Rita McGrath describes the need for companies (such as Fuji) to undertake "continuous reconfiguration." It's how companies can build the capability to move from arena to arena, rather than trying to defend existing competitive advantages. I completely agree with McGrath's assertion, and it's collective disruption that can be a key enabler for these companies to find, nurture, and incubate these new arenas in fast-changing markets. To me, first of all, the missing link in her argument is how these companies can identify the markets that are about to tip when the executives are viewing the market from the lens of their existing business. It's extremely difficult—maybe not impossible—and it takes quite the visionary and entrepreneurial executive to be able to see around corners like this. Beyond identifying the right markets and timing to enter, how do these established companies actually develop the capabilities and knowledge of these markets, aside from wholesale acquisitions of established players (and we all know how that usually turns out anyway)?

That's where the ecosystem comes in. Some very smart entrepreneurs, many of whom are corporate dropouts from these same companies, are developing new-generation technologies and businesses. They have deep understanding of their domains, and in aggregate the leaders in these emerging spaces provide an expert network (or canaries in coal the mine) regarding what technologies and designs are about to be become dominant. At least they have a much better read than the large, established corporate leaders looking to enter the space. That's why the smart move is to build and nurture a network of entrepreneurs, academia, and others to both diversify some risk and provide insights into market timing and direction.

A MODEL FOR COLLECTIVE DISRUPTION

Collective disruption is about applying many of the concepts of collaboration to the strategy of new business creation. It's about building and nurturing a network of entrepreneurs, technology startups, and other creative minds and working in concert with your internal resources in a networked approach to rapidly envision, incubate, and commercialize a pipeline of new business opportunities.

I've outlined the framework in four iterative phases summarized in Fig. 5.1:

COLLECTIVE DISRUPTION FRAMEWORK

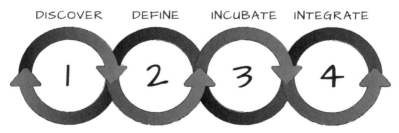

FIG. 5.1

1. Discover (Engage the Ecosystem): In this phase you'll learn the basic steps for leveraging your ecosystem to identify new business opportunities and put the concepts to work in support of your goals. The discover phase is focused on identifying the transformational opportunities relevant to your business. Begin with a customer focus and then identify the key players and the networks (as we discussed in chapter 3). It is both an outbound strategic effort and an inbound effort of assessing unforeseen opportunities brought to you. You'll need to provide seed funding and resources for these activities. What makes discovery unique in our context is the focus on providing practical ways that you and your teams can actually engage with partners in identifying breakthrough growth opportunities. Chapter 6 will help you understand the discover phase in the context of innovation ecosystems.

Example: As part of Unilever's ecosystem engagement, the company has created its Science Grid with a curated group of leading universities globally. Now the company has extended the effort with a deeper discovery partnership with the University of Liverpool in the United Kingdom. A new state-of-the-art facility co-funded by the two, plus support from government groups, is the cornerstone of an integrated and accelerated approach to R&D. Combined with its corporate venturing group, open innovation group, and other initiatives, Unilever is focused on not only leveraging external partners for technologies but also engaging with them for joint learning and early-stage exploration.

2. Define (Opportunities and Business Models): Look for the presence of a very open-ended scoping and defining activity for evaluating opportunities. This process imagines business models around the new opportunities and engages in a preliminary way with the right internal and external resources. The goal: define opportunities for an initial business opportunity through an iterative process of using these assessments to decide whether to explore further or drop. Venture capital models for opportunity screening and funding are also part of this phase, as they help guide the decision-making process and determine whether that new idea is actually a business. As we explore the define phase in chapter 7, you'll see that this can and should be a collaborative effort.

Example: Ricardo dos Santos (ex-senior director of new business at Qualcomm) shared with me how the company managed its Venture Fest program, where via an innovation challenge program internal teams identified new business opportunities and new business models. According to de Santos, "We needed breakthrough innovation and not just new R&D programs. Those things necessitated new business models and experiments." Defining these business models became part of the internal team's core efforts.

3. Incubate (Evolve and Accelerate): This is the application of a modified version of the lean methodology, tweaked for the collective disruption context. Incubation provides the opportunity to search for the right business model, to prove out the opportunity, and to evolve the opportunity until it is ready to scale.

In chapter 8 we'll discuss and provide examples of how incubation can be done in at least three ways:

- Inside-In (e.g., integrated): This model is a focus on internally managed efforts and is not mutually exclusive of the choices below. A corporate team internally manages transformative innovation efforts but has the autonomy, skills, focus, and partnerships to create breakthrough opportunities and new businesses.

- Inside-Out (e.g., accelerators): Dedicated corporate accelerators and corporate tie-ins to existing accelerators are hot trends today. We'll provide practical advice on the pros and cons of the corporate accelerator model and some examples of several variations on the model.

- Outside-In (e.g., imbedded entrepreneurs): Another model that can work is imbedding external partners and entrepreneurs in corporate ventures. It's difficult to pull off without the right entrepreneurs who can navigate the corporate landscape and avoid the landmines.

4. Integrate (Transition and Scale): From the beginning, a critical task is designing these new teams and structures as both separate and connected— islands with a bridge to the mainland. They need enough separation to allow them to operate outside of the tight financial controls of the current business. However, at the same time, they need enough engagement with the main business to ensure they're being designed for eventual integration. This is true whether they will eventually be absorbed into the existing corporate framework or spun off as something entirely new. In this phase, covered in chapter 9, the new business is parallel scaled and ultimately integrated more completely into the business. This integration could be via exercise of option agreement or, if it's already an internally owned venture, beginning to integrate the resources and business line into the parent.

Example: This is how Jarden handled the creation of its Margaritaville Frozen Concoction Maker business. First, the Margaritaville team was set up as a completely separate business incubation team, independent from the core business priorities, structures, and reporting lines. As the initial products were launched and succeeded in the market, Jarden began to integrate the product line, first from a market-facing standpoint (sales) and then finally incorporating the business into the existing appliance business unit. This is a good example of treating the organization of these business incubation efforts differently at each stage of their life cycle.

ASOKA VEERAVAGU,
VP NEW BUSINESS DEVELOPMENT, JARDEN CONSUMER SOLUTIONS

Jarden Consumer Solutions is one of the largest consumer products businesses you've never heard of. But you know its leading brands, including Sunbeam, Oster, Mr. Coffee, Crock-Pot, and many other household brand names. Asoka Veeravagu explains how its Transformational Innovation team champions new business creation and how it balances autonomy and integration.

The Transformational Innovation (TI) team charter is to identify, develop, incubate, and then eventually launch new business creation opportunities that are outside of our core—out further from where we traditionally excel as a company. We have been focused on new business creation at Jarden Consumer Solutions for the past 10 years.

TI's role within the company is to really focus on whitespace growth opportunities, going after new ideas that are far from core, very different from our current business model, and that can be highly transformative for the organization.

The success of this separate TI team stems from four key drivers. First, we have a small, fully committed team, with 100% dedicated resources, not shared with other parts of the organization, so we're not getting 20% of people's time here, 50% there. We're a focused core team that's made up of people who possess a "corporate entrepreneurial mindset." The team is empowered to think and act like a startup, to move nimbly, to try different things, to have a higher tolerance for risk and failure. At the same time they understand that we're operating within a larger public company and we do have processes and procedures, accountability, and information flow. Having team members who are comfortable with that corporate entrepreneurial mindset has been really key.

Second, we have dedicated funding, so we're not siphoning investment from other business initiatives. Our innovation team has a dedicated budget that's planned and set aside every year. Our executive team approves the budget and essentially acts as quasi-venture capitalists. We uncover the opportunities, demonstrate progress, and they, in turn, release funds. We are held accountable for prudent investment and for proving out the revenue and profit potential of the innovation initiatives in our portfolio.

Another key element for success is the support and alignment we have from our executive leadership team. We report directly to the executive leadership of the company, so we're not a skunk-works team tucked into a business unit, where we may be competing for resources or starved for funding or people if times get tough. The initiatives we are working on are for the purpose of furthering our long-term corporate business objectives. And all key members of the management team are aligned and supportive of our priorities.

Aside from our separation from the core, a final key element of our success is collaboration. We work highly collaboratively with the business units to identify which opportunity spaces to prioritize and develop into new business initiatives. So we address areas that business teams have identified as important to accomplish their five-year business goals. While they remain focused developing initiatives to introduce in years one and two, we focus on making progress on initiatives to fill the pipeline in years three to five. Not only do we align on opportunity spaces that are important but also we have a business unit champion as a member of the core team. The champion may not be actively involved in the day-to-day creation of these new business initiatives, but he or she is very involved in the direction, key decisions, and integration with the core business in the future. So we're not operating in isolation by any means.

Yes, challenges will always exist around new business creation within any company. One is the risk tolerance for true whitespace opportunity creation. These are high-risk, high-reward initiatives, but if a company's corporate culture is more risk averse, then it leads to smaller, more incremental bets. To avoid focusing solely on incremental opportunities, we map out and manage a balanced innovation portfolio. Some opportunities are going to be small, quick bets that serve a specific business purpose or goal, and we can do many more of those. Then there are the big-bet, truly game-changing ideas. They're high risk, with high reward if done correctly. They're going to need a lot of investment, resources, and a longer time horizon, but we've vetted them, so the big bets we're placing are on opportunities that have the potential to be truly transformational.

Another challenge is having the patience that's necessary to adequately incubate new businesses. In the transformational space, the definition and measures of success can vary widely within an organization. That's why we work to set expectations and ground our executive *team on where we should expect to be within a specific time frame. It's really about establishing the right initial trajectory for the long-term success of the business. A new incubating business may be small and remain in the test-and-learn phase for quite some time while we're proving the business model assumptions and building a scalable model. We focus on progress milestones rather than "how big will it be and how fast will it get there." By setting the right expectations and tracking achievement against established goals, given the type of initiative, we're improving our patience for the incubation period to develop appropriately.*

An important part of our team's mission is to help shift the organization's thinking from conventional approaches. We do this a number of ways. Rather than focusing on our current product portfolio and innovating within that space, we focus on consumer "jobs to be done." We ask, "What jobs are the consumers trying to accomplish in their life?" Even more broadly, What is the opportunity space or hunting ground that we're interested in going after, for example. beverages at home. As a hunting ground, this gives us a much wider area of exploration. Then we take a deep dive into consumer "jobs to be done" in this space, and only at that stage do we identify new product and business opportunities.

To develop transformational spaces, obviously, you have to venture into unknown areas that have high uncertainty and ambiguity and, hence, risk. Often, these initiatives may require unique skills and capabilities that are outside our core areas of expertise. We've openly engaged with outside partners and experts who bring complementary skill sets and capabilities to help us navigate, get smart, and develop new businesses and new products in these spaces. It's been another key element of success for us. If we take a purely internal approach, we'll get only so far, but by opening up our doors and stepping beyond our four walls, we can achieve so much more.

Asoka Veeravagu is vice president of new business development for Jarden Consumer Solutions, a division of Jarden Corporation, a leading provider of a diverse range of consumer products with a portfolio of more than 120 trusted, quality brands sold globally.

BENEFITS AND CHALLENGES

The collective disruption framework has many benefits:

- Everyone plays to his or her strengths. I said earlier that you can't just call a meeting and order everyone to innovate. At the same time, you can't walk into a Silicon Valley startup and demand that everyone develop a national marketing campaign dovetailing with the goals of three of your existing corporate brands. Smart people tend to be specialists, and collective disruption taps those specialties. It allows the external innovators to dream and create while allowing the corporate managers to remain coordinated and planned. The system acknowledges that a great company thrives on a variety of skill sets, and an open ecosystem can embrace them all.

- The collective disruption framework allows for the right talents and resources to come together as needed and for a fluid sense of flexibility to course though the new business process. At times teams may be together 24-7; at other times those individuals will be assigned elsewhere. Rather than create a situation in which departments or business units manage silos of talent, this new ecosystem collaboration model allows talent to come together and drift apart as needed.

- The framework aligns with the evolving mobile workforce of today (and tomorrow). Increasingly, the days of one-company careers, or even one career, are over. Success used to mean getting a "good" job at a "good" company and working there until the day you got your gold watch and retired to Arizona. Not anymore. Today, workers expect to move from company to company, even from industry to industry—certainly not sitting around in any one place too long. The collective disruption concept supports this on-the-move workforce.

- Collective disruption provides a much more efficient value creation market. Today, entrepreneurs try new ideas that may or may not find an exit (or success). Collective disruption allows the ideas to be explored and tested in a robust and efficient way. This model reverse engineers the process to ensure that the ventures that are nurtured are customer driven and have a potential home in these large companies.

To be sure, the system also has its challenges:

- It compounds control and intellectual property issues. Who owns the idea? Who is first in line for the payoff? Who's on the hook in the case of a lawsuit? These are easy issues to address when dealing with either a company or a startup. But when collective disruption creates an ecosystem fluid with hybrid arrangements, the lines blur. Sorting out the legal issues around these approaches can be a complicated process.

- It mixes cultural mindsets. While it sounds exciting to have young innovative technologists sitting down with your brand manager, keep in mind that those two mindsets aren't always a match. Managing communication between the cultures and facilitating an environment of mutual respect are key challenges.

- You don't own the talents you nurture and influence toward your goals. In the end, the truth must be faced: your ecosystem does not work for you. You may have contracts that bind you, memos of understanding, licensing agreements. But, ultimately, that talent may take a new direction without you one day. It is a risk that the old walled castle R&D approach never had to face, but it is a truism of the new landscape.

To face these challenges, traditional companies will need to sharpen their entrepreneurial skills. They'll need to learn to collaborate better. This is a mandate for the organization and for the individuals within it. Collaboration is the hallmark of the startup culture, and companies that want to participate in collective disruption will need to play by those rules.

If information and ideas are coming from new sources, the old funnel system may not be appropriate. A wider web of corporate connectivity will need to be drawn. Corporate players used to hierarchy will need to adjust to the updated flow charts.

Collective disruption is ultimately about marrying the best of two previously disconnected worlds. The VCs were the ones who typically bridged these worlds by providing funding to startups and often connecting them for strategic exits with corporates years later. Collective disruption is about creating a much more efficient market for leveraging the unique vision and skills of the entrepreneur with the marketing and distribution scale of the corporate executive.

It's really reverse engineering for both parties. By linking the strategic needs of corporates with early-stage startup development, the probability is much higher that the venture will be one that meets consumer needs and the strategic needs of the corporate partner that will eventually scale it. Corporations' early engagement with entrepreneurs not only helps them guide the development of these big ideas but also begins to educate and equip them with the skills and attitudes necessary to integrate the startup successfully without killing the magic. It's not easy, but those who figure out how to do this well will be the absolute market leaders.

Cisco has paid over $2 billion over two decades to acquire the startups of a trio of serial entrepreneurs (Mario Mazzola, Prem Jain and Luca Cafiero). In each of at least three ventures, Cisco was the sole investor and then acquired each spin-in as they were ready to scale. Nuovo Systems was founded with a $70+ million investment from Cisco in 2006. Then Cisco acquired the business for $678 million two years later. Crazy? Perhaps, but the Unified Computing Systems (UCS) servers category that this created is now nearly a $3 billion business for Cisco. Cisco is leveraging these and other entrepreneurs to co-create the future of Cisco.

I've made the case for a new approach and introduced a framework for collective disruption. Now, in this next chapter, let's go deeper into the first of these phases, discover.

6

DISCOVER: ENGAGE THE ECOSYSTEM

DISCOVER

As you develop your own innovation networks and get more plugged into the larger ecosystems relevant to your business and industry, you'll be able to reap benefits for both core business reinvention and new business development. You're developing a very strong pipeline of ideas and a very deep bench for entrepreneurial talent if you do it right. What we're talking about here is forging a unique partnership between large companies and entrepreneurs that benefits each.

In this chapter, we'll lay out the basic framework for leveraging your ecosystem to identify new business opportunities and put the concepts to work in support of your goals. In chapter 3, we emphasized the importance of nurturing and engaging with networks of innovators relevant to your business and your categories. In this chapter, we'll provide more practical advice and tactics for bringing this to life for new business creation.

MY OWN EXPERIENCE

In 2009, I was involved in an exciting and challenging opportunity related to applying mobile technology to brand building and marketing for leading companies. I launched and led a mobile technology consortium called Third Screen Marketplace, right when mobile was tipping into the omnipresent phenomenon we all take for granted today. In the early months as we were searching for the right business model, I spoke with chief marketing officers of more than a dozen leading global brands. Ten of these companies were among the top 25 advertisers in the world, and none of them were spending more than a few percentage points of their budgets on mobile. They were still heavily tilted toward traditional media. Thanks to the pull of our cofounder and advisor, Jim Stengel, ex-CMO of Procter & Gamble, I was granted unusual access to this high-level CMO community.

What I learned from these discussions was that these big brands were lost on several fronts. First, they were struggling with how to leverage mobile in a bigger way. These were smart, experienced executives. They knew instinctively that mobile was big, and they didn't want to be left behind. Yet they were doing little more than sprinkling a few investments. They had a collection of small-scale pilots across a hodgepodge of mobile startups, ad agency initiatives, and collaborative projects with major mobile providers such as Google and Nokia.

Second, these companies had no real strategy or criteria for separating the good from the bad among the many startups that were granted meetings and demonstrations with the marketing teams. Without a clear filter, how could they select the best digital patners? In the absence of that, they resorted to a strategy of "show high interest and then stall" as a way to corner and keep as many options alive as they could, while they tried to assess which would be the winning or dominant designs of the near future. A parade of possibilities filed by: how to assess location-based services for contextual advertising, how to integrate into retailers' point-of-sale systems and avoid fraud with mobile coupons, how to build the large-scale product information databases that could provide real-time information for consumers at shelf and the opportunities to promote complementary products—the list goes on. It was pure chaos. It was the Wild West.

With Third Screen Marketplace (3SM), we built a consortium of some of these leading brands and led cross-company programs (noncompetitive in each particular project) to help them make sense of this market and identify opportunities where collaboration could make a difference. We did it by putting the consumer at the center of our work and using proprietary methods to develop a deep understanding of the consumer's journey. Suzanne Tosolini, an ex-P&G digital marketer who led 3SM's consumer insights, directed our efforts to uncover deep consumer needs across mind, body, soul, and task. In the period of about six months, we and our brand partners developed an in-depth understanding of consumers around mobile and how mobile could provide real utility for these consumers and loyalty to the brands delivering new services on mobile.

That's where the magic happened. When we had a foundation built upon deep understanding of consumers and their mobile experiences and then layered that with the strategic needs of these brands, really important new insights and opportunities surfaced. We used that as a filter to engage with a broad range of the innovation ecosystem within the mobile industry. The brands involved in this venture were premier brands you would know, so we had no trouble getting the attention of startups and their venture backers.

For one of the major projects, we undertook the big and promising—but confusing—prospects for mobile-enabled shopping. We identified more than 200 technologies, a list that was changing almost daily as the market evolved. But engaging with these startups through the lens of consumer needs (and brand needs) brought amazing clarity, almost ease, to our task of narrowing this down to the short list of potential technology partners for pilots and co-development.

Just as powerfully, these startups were eager to finally understand the end game for these brands and to be privy to the consumer insights we brought to them. They had been just as frustrated as the big companies with the previous ad hoc process. This new system offered more promise.

It was an exciting time to be part of this collaboration and the cross learning that took place during these explorations and pilots.

We organized demo days in different cities to find and vet a select group of entrepreneurs directly with our brand partners. The short list companies (seven, in the case of mobile shopping) were brought together for pilots to test new aggregated platforms with consumers.

Our goal with 3SM was to ultimately co-create new business ventures with these brand companies to allow them to scale the right technologies much faster and bring consumer focus to accelerate mobile brand building.

So, were we successful? Yes and no.

We were highly successful in creating new consumer understanding and in driving valuable new partnerships between our brand members and with the selected startups, but (not surprisingly in hindsight) when the time came, we could not get the brands to co-invest in the opportunities. They ended up pursuing their own solutions and leveraging many of the technologies and partners we brought to them.

Here's another measure of success. Of the seven technology companies we identified as critical players in a mobile shopping platform we envisioned, five were acquired within a year of our mobile shopping project. As the market progressed, these startups' fit with consumer and strategic needs eventually became obvious to others as well.

Perhaps most important is what we learned in the process: both big brands and startups want an end to the inefficient process of searching for collaboration partners and ad hoc approaches to selecting platforms and technologies. We learned that there is tremendous power in directly engaging these two disparate groups in focusing the best of the brands and the best of the technology providers on co-creating solutions against real consumer needs.

How can you be part of that convergence and mutual benefit? The rest of the chapter will focus on that.

STRATEGIC INTENT FOR DISCOVERY

If we want to apply this network concept specifically to the task of new business creation (as opposed to sourcing of ideas for incremental product or service improvements), the key first step is ensuring we're clear on our goals. Too often companies start to look for partners and technologies without a clear understanding of why they are looking and what they're looking for. That said, you shouldn't be setting out detailed plans and objectives based on some preconceived notion of what you're trying to create. Keep it broad, because these types of strategic growth initiatives will likely need to pivot along the way.

In the world of collective disruption, strategy is emergent, not fixed. Certainly, discovery happens when the foundational elements of strategy are in place, but more detailed plans emerge based on rapidly learning and evolving markets.

Henry Mintzberg, author of *The Rise and Fall of Strategic Planning*, argues that strategy emerges over time as intentions collide with and accommodate a changing reality. Emergent strategy, he says, is a set of actions, or behavior, consistent over time, "a realized pattern [that] was not expressly intended" in the original strategic planning. Nowhere is this more true or necessary than in the worlds of startups and new business creation, where, as Steve Blank, a successful Silicon Valley entrepreneur, investor, and writer, says, "No business plan survives the first interaction with a customer."

"EMERGENT" STRATEGY

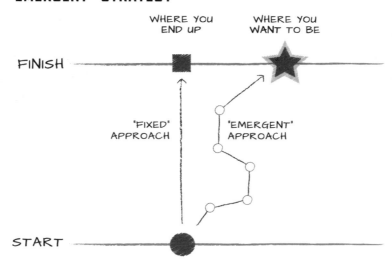

FIG. 6.1

An emergent strategy doesn't mean flying blindly. As illustrated in Fig. 6.1, it's simply a much more dynamic and realistic way to plan in this environment we're talking about here, where so much is shifting around us. We're kidding ourselves to think we can predict the future or anticipate which technology will become dominant or which of the many platforms the consumers will choose. Scott Cook, CEO of Intuit, said, "For every one of our failures, we had spreadsheets that looked awesome." Don't create beautiful spreadsheets for the wrong strategy. Develop strategies that you can adjust as you learn and the market evolves.

Here's an example. When my consulting firm was helping a major pharma company develop commercialization plans for a unique antiviral flu mask (including H1N1), we didn't know when or whether the market might tip and become a consumer market. At the time, and still today, the primary market was in government stockpiling for epidemic preparedness, with limited opportunities in the healthcare provider industry.

In evaluating the consumer market, we asked ourselves, when might it become socially acceptable for populations to wear these masks in public places? We're already seeing this happen at a much faster rate in Asia, where pollution and compact populations have driven their use. Mask use is also much more common and accepted in Japan, China, Korea, and other Asian markets than in the West. Remember the last time you saw someone wearing a mask in a mall or on an airplane here in the United States? You see it as an oddity, and chances are the person who's wearing that mask is from Asia and is doing so to protect himself or herself (or others) from transmitting viruses and germs.

We could theorize that a major pandemic (the next H1N1 equivalent at a larger scale) might be the kind of catalyst to change behavior both during the event and perhaps for the long term. Bottom line: we couldn't predict when the consumer market might emerge in a meaningful way for these products. Our strategy? Focus on the institutional market that exists today (governments, hospitals) but create a limited beachhead product and business for the consumer market. In this way, we'd have a product ready and be able to react more quickly to scale up a consumer business versus waiting for strong demand and only then going through the FDA approval process and retail sell-in process.

HAPPY HUNTING

With strategic intent clear, what's needed next is the development of a number of primary hunting grounds. We are not talking about detailed problem briefs, as are often the process in technology scouting, but rather about broad opportunity areas.

What's a hunting ground? It's a focus area that's defined by a set of related opportunities that can fuel a line of products or hopefully a whole new business. For Jarden Consumer Solutions, a good hunting ground was for new opportunities related to casual entertaining. Jarden created a new standalone business around the Margaritaville Frozen Concoction Maker and other entertaining-related products and consumables and grew it from nothing into an incremental $80+ million within just a few years.

Key elements of an attractive hunting ground:

- It is defined in part by a set of consumers or customers (the who) and a set of unmet needs (the opportunity)

- Market gaps are already observed and current players aren't adequately addressing current and emerging needs

- It is narrow enough and actionable enough to enable efficient focus of resources to develop and identify solutions

- It is broad enough to encompass a variety of opportunities and not a single product solution

P&G uses a different model of discovery and engagement by putting key resources in innovation hotbeds such as Silicon Valley. As part of its Corporate Platforms organization, these resources are charged with engaging with the ecosystem of startups and venture capitalists that they could never develop deep relationships with from Cincinnati. In one example, they have developed a very deep and synergistic relationship with Kleiner Perkins Caufield & Byers (KPCB), the famous Sand Hill Road VC in Silicon Valley. KPCB gains access for its portfolio of companies in designing and scaling them in alignment with P&G brand needs, including collaborative pilots. P&G gains early looks at promising emerging ideas and puts them in the flow of technology coming out of Silicon Valley that may be relevant to its digital marketing efforts.

In the case of Shopkick, P&G actually imbedded one of its executives, Sonny Jandial, for one and a half years in this location-based marketing firm, even though P&G didn't have a direct investment in the company. Both parties gained from the deep interaction. Cyriac Roeding, CEO and cofounder of Shopkick said, "Shopkick and P&G Corporate Platforms have developed one of the most unique partnerships between the Silicon Valley–based innovation world and the brand world. And after 6 months in the market, Shopkick reached 1 million users. P&G helped us get there through our powerful partnership."

Jandial shared with me the challenge of gaining engagement and support within P&G: "When you're talking about these things that are so dependent on a major shift, you end up being the person who is trying to communicate where the puck is going. For a lot of large companies, it's a hard thing when you're betting on the future and not on where it is today. You're trying to enroll other stakeholders who live in the present and live in what they're doing today. They look at the number and say, 'Twenty percent mobile phone penetration? I'm going to wait because it's not big enough for me.'" It was Jandial's credibility within P&G, including having been the brand manager on the original Swiffer, that helped him gain support from P&G brands to engage with Shopkick.

Local resources and collaborations such as Shopkick provide P&G with an ear to the ground and an ability to form deeper relationships that help in its larger mission of discovering and leveraging Silicon Valley's emerging technologies.

STARTUPS AS SENSING NETWORKS

If you've developed a strong working relationship with entrepreneurial firms relevant to the areas in which you are exploring, you may find another benefit: you can leverage their collective knowledge to better understand market trends in the areas where they play and provide early warning of key activities and trends.

Be thoughtful and strategic in building relationships with individual companies, accelerators, and venture capital firms in the areas that you believe will matter to your road maps. These relationships can inform your strategy as well as provide ongoing intelligence regarding evolving technologies and even when a market might be about to tip. But it's not all about taking; you need to give as well. These must be two-way relationships, and the startup communities you engage with can benefit greatly from your understanding of the consumer and your company's future needs.

The trust and communication that are built through this two-way process are what pave the way for deeper collaboration down the road.

PUT THE CUSTOMER (OR CONSUMER) AT THE CENTER

Everything starts with the customer (or the consumer, if you're B2C). Customer development is one of the most basic yet powerful concepts in the lean startup movement. Customer development demands that founders put their technologies and proposed solutions aside (even if a concept is in development) and, independent of their ideas, ensure that they have a clear understanding of:

- Who the customer is (articulating a clear definition)

- What problem the customer faces (again with clarity)

I've done consumer insight work within and for large companies most of my career. One wouldn't think that entrepreneurs have much to teach large companies about consumer or customer research, right? But having gone through lean startup training myself and working the process as an entrepreneur, I have come to the realization that we as corporate executives still have a lot to learn about customer discovery. There's something visceral about putting aside all of the conjoint analyses, quantitative studies, and focus group results and simply getting out of the building to talk with customers directly—not just the research experts but core team members.

So, in the spirit of lean startup methods, get back to basics. Get out of the building and get face to face with customers. Find them. Talk with them. Encourage them to articulate (and validate) the problems that you think you're about to solve. When we were engaging with early mobile users during our work in Third Screen Marketplace about how they might use their mobile phones to help them with their shopping experience, we didn't start by showing them our breakthrough concepts for new mobile-enabled approaches to offers, product information, and shopping lists. We started by identifying a core group of women: female heads of household who were time starved, value conscious, and digitally/mobile savvy.

We spent a lot of time with them in one-on-one interviews and even accompanying them in their shopping to learn more about the problems and frustrations they had with their current process and experiences, everything from building shopping lists to interest and engagement in clipping coupons.

When I joined Sunbeam as VP of new product development at the start of the company's turnaround, one of the simple things I did was to encourage our engineers and designers to get out of the building to observe in-home consumer behaviors and to sit behind the glass during focus groups. I felt it critically important for the person who was going to be making those difficult trade-off decisions at 8 o'clock at night to be able to put a face to the end user and keep him or her top of mind. I believe that putting the end user at the center of everything we did and driving direct consumer interaction within our development teams were key factors in our ultimate success in a very difficult turnaround.

In defining the customer and problem, put your solutions and ideas aside for the time being. You might find it easy to structure customer interviews around getting reaction to your concepts, but all you'll likely be doing is getting the answers you want to hear. The first order of business is making sure you've identified the right customers and the right problem (or problems) to solve.

Getting out of the building to talk with customers does something else. It helps to validate in a very tangible way whether these customers who you believe are your target actually exist. If you struggle finding them in the real world for these customer development interviews, that's a hint that they may be harder to find in the numbers that you're projecting on your very thorough and beautiful spreadsheets.

CASE IN POINT: FIT & FRESH

In developing a new category of business with Fit & Fresh, a smaller entrepreneurial consumer products company focused on chilled lunch containers, my consulting team helped the company identify a new adjacent category for growth: on-the-go food transport and serving for social gatherings, including picnics, tailgates, potlucks, etc. We believed this was an underdeveloped market, and we had identified an opportunity for a whole new group of products to address a gap in the market.

We initially assumed we'd develop a line of products in this new category that were incrementally more premium priced but stayed close to their core mass price points. More importantly, we would focus on addressing some core unmet needs for these consumers—such as the consumer could take that large pan of lasagna from home to that pot-luck dinner without it spilling in his or her backseat. By getting out into customers' homes and connecting directly, we saw the workarounds the consumers were creating, such as wrapping food dishes in bath towels to prevent spills and keep food hot.

But we also discovered something else. We identified a narrowly defined segment of people (spanning millennials to boomers) who were passionate about sharing good food with friends and often on the go. This deeper understanding of the consumer helped the business team make a courageous decision to design solutions that wowed these consumers and to worry less about price point as long as we delivered important value. We introduced a line of breakthrough products, incorporating aerogel insulation technology from the aerospace industry, that enabled very sleek designs while delivering incredible performance in keeping food hot or cold for hours, twice as long as competitors. Ultimately, we successfully launched a whole new category called "Gatherings" that took the company into uncharted and profitable new territory of premium channels; we expect this to lift the value of the entire enterprise.

CHICKEN OR EGG?

No one would argue the importance of customer focus in driving innovation, yet in today's rapidly changing environment and constant influx of disruptive challengers, large companies have a real hunger to search for breakthrough technologies. So, the age-old question of consumer driven versus technology driven takes on new importance. I still often get asked about whether companies should start with identifying needs and then search for technologies that address those needs or identify compelling intellectual property and then match that with unmet consumer needs that can be solved. Which comes first?

My answer? Yes.

Huh?

What I mean by this non-answer is that the question implies a linear approach of first A and then B. Innovation, especially the transformative type, is an iterative process. The process you use for incremental product and service improvements will seldom work for real breakthroughs. Your company may do all the right consumer interviews and observational research to identify compelling unmet consumer needs, yet in spite of this excellent work, you may not be able to develop or source a compelling solution, or perhaps the competitive environment won't provide the opportunity to introduce the innovation into the market. The time just may not yet be right.

Rather, companies should be continually scanning for technologies, consumer or market trends, and marketplace opportunities. To me, it's all about finding and exploiting the intersections between unmet needs, enabling solutions (e.g., technology) and marketplace opportunities.

Compelling and winning ideas lie at these intersections. It's not about where you start but about ensuring that you're truly finding these intersections. So, if you dream up or run across a breakthrough technology or unique idea that's great, just be willing to step back from it at that point and validate the idea objectively against the consumer problem and the market opportunity.

All that said, when searching for strategic growth opportunities, I still support creating a deep understanding of consumers and their needs. Think of it as creative fuel for your innovation and growth efforts. With this fuel, you'll see potential technologies and solutions through a clearer lens and increase your chances of creating really big ideas. Just don't expect your technology scanning to solve the problem you've set out to solve. As Louis Pasteur once said, "Chance favors the prepared mind." I'd add an *open* mind.

DISCOVERING IDEAS WITHIN

We need to find the best ideas wherever they are. While I'm emphasizing discovery of externally sourced ideas, don't underestimate the power of unleashing the ideas within the enterprise. But finding disruptive ideas often requires more entrepreneurial approaches to encourage them, and it requires engaging the organization's entire talent base in the effort.

Dondeena Bradley (global head of innovation for Weight Watchers and former VP, Nutrition Ventures for Pepsico) told me, "It's hard to innovate inside a predictable system, which is why you sometimes need to disrupt things when it's time to find breakthroughs. As a student of innovation and a woman leader, I have done my share of challenging the system. I was seeing, firsthand, people's desire to work together in new ways and their discomfort in leaving traditional structures. It became clear that collaboration requires different tools and styles of leadership. I began to wonder about the possibility of bringing more empathy and emotional intelligence into the process. Personally, I'm hopeful, because I think that sharing knowledge and working for the greater good are a collaborative—and in many ways disruptive—approach that many women leaders naturally know how to do."

Success in collective disruption requires a focus on inclusion of a diverse group of creative minds both inside and outside the enterprise. Discovery programs that allow ideas to emerge through sources outside of the core new product and service development function can accelerate it.

Here's how Ricardo dos Santos used an internal venture boot camp to leverage Qualcomm's talented employee base. It surfaced emerging opportunities to help make sure the company didn't miss out on important market trends.

RICARDO DOS SANTOS,
EX-SENIOR DIRECTOR OF NEW BUSINESS DEVELOPMENT AT QUALCOMM

How can you get an entire organization to step up and explore new venture opportunities—and incorporate lean principles along the way? Dos Santos started a boot camp.

I joined Qualcomm from a startup that was acquired by Qualcomm and found a role in new business development. Eventually, I created an original innovation program called the Qualcomm Venture Fest. It was a way to crowdsource ideas from anywhere in the company. It was also an idea accelerator and a way to do innovation training contextually.

I explicitly didn't want to compete with the core business or some obvious adjacencies. I called our work breakthrough innovation, and I painted a typical growth matrix along technology access and a new market access and said, "We're the program that's supposed to push some things out."

We went from a standalone online idea tournament (I'd call it our minimum viable product) into something that combined an offline effort to turn top ideas into actionable, investment-worthy projects—an idea development boot camp. We encouraged employees to practice "entrepreneurial thinking and behaviors" to prove their idea's financial and strategic potential. The program retained its tournament structure, where 10 to 20 ideas out of hundreds of original entries would make it to this boot camp round, and this was the heart of the program.

The first day of boot camp, people were instructed to recruit a small venture team. They were advised on how to round off their (founder) skills, expertise, personality, and connections with those of complementary team members. It was also critical to think ahead in terms of where they thought their idea would eventually need to be internally validated, improved, and supported. Based on this, they could recruit the appropriate mentors.

It was a grassroots, volunteer effort. Our program simply made it more efficient for deserving "intrapreneurs" to get their "day in court." It welcomed all, but the rigorous tournament and boot camp phases filtered out the less committed change makers. It provided context for "founder types" to recruit a small team of volunteers, enlist upper management mentorship, receive training, and use modest amounts of seed funding to think through and validate their ideas before "pitching" them to the company's CEO and the rest of his executive staff.

I was always telling those who joined my program that we needed to innovate like startups (I admired their boldness, speed, and resourcefulness). Bottom-up innovators could relate: they shared the same discontent for complacency but realized that when it came to their own blue-sky ideas, the burden of proof rested with them—startups offered a model for self-empowerment, albeit at a different risk/reward profile.

Someone pointed out that there was a flaw in using startups as the corporate entrepreneur's ideal: we could try to innovate like startups, but how, exactly, did startups innovate? Why did so many fail?

So we had inspiration but not substance in our teachings to employees. I really didn't have an answer until I first bumped into the term "the lean startup." I was trained as an industrial engineer, and I knew about lean manufacturing, which was about cutting out extraneous fat such as inventory, defects, long cycle times, etc. What was the analogous "fat" in startups? When finally pointed to Steve Blank's and Eric Ries's writings, I was like, "Aha! Now you're talking!"

We took the major principles and applied them to our particular situation; we become more specific about what the teams should be learning and doing in the boot camp. We asked them to reconsider their ideas by separating the problem from the solution and to generate additional alternatives (for both). We asked them to first test the problem with their intended customers to sharpen their hypothesis and then start testing their solutions iteratively through prototypes and demos.

We completely revamped how teams pitched, being upfront with what they learned and what was left to learn through continued experiments. The "Let's just go for it! Are you with me?" stance was replaced by a cost/benefit conversation of "If you invest in this next stage of risk, I'll bring this back as a reward (option, strategic, and exit value), and then we'll see whether it's worth proceeding to the next stage."

The lean approach encouraged the company to make small bets in many more directions than traditional "business as usual" would have dictated. Usually, making decisions on large upfront investments in the absence of proof of concept results in passive or aggressive resistance to unloosen any purse strings. Venture Fest broadened our view. Augmented reality, spin-transfer torque chips, wearables, vehicle-to-vehicle communication, ultra-low-power server chips, and other ideas were embedded in the Qualcomm collective mind by the Venture Fest upstarts.

I remember our CEO saying to one of the Venture Fest teams a few years back: "This vehicle-to-vehicle wireless mesh stuff is a great idea that could one day put an end to deadly auto accidents. I hadn't realized it has so much in common with some of the technical challenges we've solved in other areas. I'm glad you guys brought this up now!" Then he turned around and asked his executive staff what they thought. The head of R&D raised his hand and said: "I'll take this one. Let's learn more." In this case, the Venture Fest project lead brought tremendous credibility. He had just joined Qualcomm after completing seminal university research on V2V communications.

Qualcomm immediately formed a task force to determine where to play and whom to partner with in the connected-car arena— a typical example of how we were able to surface new ideas that became important programs we might have otherwise missed.

Ricardo dos Santos is a director with 4inno, an innovation consultancy, and a mentor for Cisco's EIR Program. Until 2012 he was a senior director of new business development with Qualcomm; dos Santos's passion is helping large companies return to their entrepreneurial roots.

SOWING SEEDS

You may engage in a very natural tendency to want to prioritize your best strategic opportunities and pick just a few for pursuit. While I'm a big believer in focus for corporate initiatives, I think a mindset shift is necessary in this context. Think more like a VC, where you need to sow a lot of seeds and spread your bets effectively for new business creation.

Real leverage is available to you if you do it right. I know a senior executive at a consumer durables company who is in charge of new business creation activities. The company's process to date is a good one, with one exception. While the individual initiatives under way are generally strong, the company mindset in selecting and starting on the next ones is still something that assumes internal development and processes.

I've challenged their thinking and have encouraged decision makers to stop trying to pick two or three and focus on them and instead pick eight to 10 and sow seeds more broadly with external partners that can prove them out. VCs don't try to pick the winning solution upfront; they spread their bets much more broadly and let the market and the entrepreneurs' efforts prove out the best. Only when the market is proven do they double down on larger investments to scale up the best. I'm not talking about a shotgun approach. Opportunities should definitely be vetted and grounded in emerging needs and aligned with future strategy. Just don't try to pick the winners upfront.

FEELING LUCKY?

Discovery is nonlinear. Don't expect it to be as simple as defining problems and finding solutions. Linear thinking works well for simple problems and systems, but as complexity increases, these approaches can fail. Innovation is complex. Discovery for disruption and new business creation is even more complex: more players, fast paced, hard to predict. If you use linear thinking in nonlinear situations, then expect to be surprised—and not necessarily in a good way.

The truth is you can't always predict when a consumer need will be uncovered or when the marketplace opportunity will present itself. Likewise, you can't always predict when or from where external opportunities might emerge. That's why you need a model of discovery that's, well, open.

So, the last point I want to leave you with in discussing discovery is that it's not all about strategy or process. It's also about mindset. Dr. Richard Wiseman conducted a study some years back that he talks about in his book *The Luck Factor*. It illustrates the point. The study was focused on self-reported lucky and unlucky people. You know these people. Which are you? You know the ones who always seem to have good luck, and good things always seem to happen for them? I know a few of the other types, too—always complaining that a black cloud must be following them.

In the study, each of these groups was shown a newspaper and asked to count the number of pictures. On average, the self-reported unlucky people spent about two minutes on the exercise, while self-reported lucky people spent seconds. Why? Lucky people tended to spot the message on page two, in big type: "Stop counting: there are 43 photos in this newspaper." In fact, the unlucky people tended to miss not only this message but also the next one about halfway through: "Stop counting. Tell the experimenter you saw this and win $250."

The lesson? Unlucky people miss opportunities because they're too busy looking for something else. Lucky people see what is there, not just what they're looking for. Open your mind and see what's there, not just what you're looking for, if you want to find the real opportunities for innovation, partners, and disruption.

When you invest the effort in creating and working your own ecosystem, you will find the opportunities. Others will call it luck, but you will know the steps you took to make that luck happen to you rather than the next person.

As we've seen, the process is neither quick nor straightforward. My own experience with Third Screen Marketplace included a substantial amount of trial and error. But this kind of innovation rewards those willing to learn on the fly. What I've discussed here so far is the first set of actions, the first steps. You'll need to take them together to understand the wider possibilities of your ecosystem.

Going forward, we'll discuss another set of steps to take in pursuit of success.

7

DEFINE: OPPORTUNITIES AND BUSINESS MODELS

How do big ideas become well-defined collaborative business opportunities? In this and upcoming chapters we'll attack this challenge and try to demystify the process. It's certainly not kismet. Defining ventures or strategic growth platforms that will eventually be a partnership means that engagement happens earlier, even in constructing the opportunity. Creating new sources of growth almost always entails business model innovation. In this chapter, we'll introduce a tool to help you explore alternative business models quickly.

To define and pursue high-risk opportunities require challenging some closely held assumptions. Many large companies approach the concept of opportunity with a lot of confidence in their existing process. After all, you don't get to be big without developing some good opportunity-spotting skills.

But as I have presented in previous chapters, the world has changed, and the climate and demands of opportunity definition have shifted around the big-company community. Defining opportunities in today's business climate demands a deeper understanding of potential partnerships (at the bare minimum) and often more direct collaboration between established companies and startups at every stage of the new business creation process. It's not your father's opportunity definition process.

Definition is a tricky stage because for many companies, the vision of success is now visible—before us like a jewel in the cave. The question now becomes how to snatch up that jewel and possess the treasure without bringing the whole cave crashing down.

For anyone who has made a misstep in a big-company innovation effort, this potential for mistakes is very real. It is what keeps so many potential big-company innovators frozen in place: what if I move forward in the wrong direction or with the wrong construct? It could blow this whole opportunity to bits before it even gets started.

ENGAGING PARTNERS IN OPPORTUNITY DEFINITION

More often than not, companies follow one of two paths if confronting a technology-driven opportunity:

- They move quickly to tie up the technology and make a bet that it's going to deliver what's promised and the market will want it.

- They stall by trying to keep the technology partner engaged and interested, but they make no commitment.

I'm offering you a third path: engage directly with these partners in defining the opportunity. It sounds scary, and there is risk, but the rewards usually outweigh both.

Engaging your external partners in co-creating or at least vetting new business models and new business creation is a strategy that both strengthens the relationship and proves out the opportunity in new ways that can benefit all parties.

Many books have been written and frameworks published on structuring alliances and partnerships. Many models are valid, and I like two in particular. The first is Alliance Management Group's alliance framework, which structures the challenge as overcoming the "three alliances in one" problem. Simply put, every alliance is really three separate but interrelated relationships. Beyond the obvious relationship between the two firms, the internal relationships at each firm between the alliance team and the broader organizational stakeholders must also be managed.

The second is from a book by Steve Steinhilber, a VP at Cisco Systems. Cisco does strategic alliances extremely well, especially customer co-development. In his book *Strategic Alliances: Three Ways to Make Them Work*, Steinhilber outlines the frameworks, organization, and relationship considerations that are critical for success.

Even with these excellent approaches, I've seen too much effort devoted to deals where the true value creation hasn't yet been quantified and the working relationship hasn't been tested. Often, too much attention is focused on the relationship at the expense of a focus on the external market opportunity. That's why I promote the idea of "externally focused" alliance development. Rather than you and your potential partners sitting in a conference room negotiating who gets what, start with an external perspective.

Here is an example from my own experience.

I previously mentioned the Weight Management Collaborative, where I helped create and facilitate a consortium of major brands. It was quite a diverse group: GSK, Kraft, Microsoft, WebMD, Reebok, Omron, and other major players in addition to a group of emerging growth companies in the space.

In our initial exploratory summits with these companies, we surfaced themes of common interest. Then we used an approach we called "collective insights" where we structured collaborative programs around these important weight management topics. We identified themes such as "family focused" and "empowered employees" and then negotiated simple teaming agreements with a set of interested companies to explore these areas. The teaming agreements laid out goals for each initiative and the roles of each company in the work. What was unique about these programs was that they were externally facing and focused on learning without predetermining longer-term partnering arrangements. Most were focused on studying consumer needs and the market opportunities and were aimed at learning (together) whether and how these themed areas could surface new business opportunities for the players.

WHAT'S MINE IS MINE

One key element we had to address in the Weight Management Collaborative was intellectual property. The initial summits we conducted were without any agreements in place. When we were then moving to exploring opportunities externally, we structured the teaming agreements to be fairly simple documents but ensured that any I/P brought in by a player remained that player's. While the focus of these pilots was in consumer studies, we protected for the potential of new joint I/P being created. The teaming agreements outlined that each player involved (remember that these were complementary companies, each in different market segments) would be granted royalty-free rights to any new I/P created for the markets in which each player currently competed.

With these ground rules in place, the collaborative was able to facilitate a series of pilots and studies where these peer companies were learning together about the opportunities in the market. After just a few months of efforts, we were able to clearly identify where the best opportunities were (and weren't) for collaborative efforts beyond the pilots. Then a more traditional alliance model kicked in, and we could develop joint development agreements with the appropriate players to continue to pursue the best ideas.

Companies face a common dilemma in deciding when to formalize agreements with entrepreneurs and how early to negotiate terms of a co-development agreement or license agreement in advance or create option rights. In these early explorations, 90% of the time they aren't going to progress, anyway. Yet, companies don't want to leave things open-ended, where the company may have added a lot of value and then it tries to tie it up and the price has gone way up. Tim Howe (until recently VP, general counsel, and head of acquisitions and licensing for Sanofi Pasteur) told me, "Part of the challenge is bridging the expectations gap. Approaches that include back-end loaded contingency deals and earn-outs have a lot of appeal and a lot of potential. But management needs to understand it can reduce your flexibility over time because now you have responsibilities to these partners."

Howe continues, "Issues in a co-development agreement tend to arise from overly optimistic and unrealistic estimates of the time and expense of running the collaboration, from start to finish. Small companies often want to develop their competencies and build infrastructure so they can become independent, controlling manufacturing, distribution, sales, etc. They often underestimate the challenges they will face and tend, generally, to be optimistic. In contrast, large companies tend to be too conservative and pessimistic; they've dealt firsthand with many of the setbacks that the startups can't begin to appreciate."

There's no simple answer, but I do believe that too many companies miss opportunities for collaboration and co-development because of an overfocus on negotiating final deals before anyone has determined whether the collaboration has value from the customer's perspective. That's how these externally focused pilots can help you more quickly validate the opportunity before proceeding to detailed negotiations. Howe also shared with me this: "What you really want to do is develop an environment where you can really trust one another, share data, and not hold back."

Intellectual property concerns remain near the top of the list of CEOs' and corporate leaders' reluctance to engage earlier and more deeply with entrepreneurial firms. Anecdotes abound about inventors suing companies for ideas they claim were theirs and inventors telling their own stories of helping companies co-develop products only to be dropped late in development once they've shared significant knowledge with their corporate partners. I won't argue that these nightmare scenarios don't happen on occasion, but I would argue that the visionary leaders I work with understand that, today, the benefits of co-creation definitely outweigh the risks.

Kate O'Keeffe (who leads Cisco's Hyper-Innovation Living Labs) shared her perspective on the trade-off between I/P protection and collaborative co-creation with partners and customers and the importance of speed. In one example she cited, "There was a dilemma in which, if we pause to develop a thorough intellectual property strategy and detailed agreement on joint ownership, it might take 12 weeks or more from a fast-moving and important customer collaboration. In this case we made the decision to proceed in parallel. Did Cisco have perfectly clear I/P protection in this instance? No, it didn't. However, we were successful in delivering a unique customer co-creation project that has been tremendous for both organizations."

Here are a few examples of how others are finding ways through the intellectual property conundrum.

- Back in 2006, General Mills' standard response to requests by outside technology providers was essentially, "It is General Mills' policy not to review, accept, or fund any submitted idea from outside the company." Just a few years later, CEO Ken Powell included this personal note on the company's new open innovation portal: "We believe that there is a great opportunity for us to enhance and accelerate our innovation efforts by teaming up with world-class innovators from outside our company." General Mills manages the idea submission effort with a simple disclosure release that ensures that initial information shared is nonconfidential. Only after preliminary reviews will it sign a confidentiality agreement.

- In similar fashion, Procter & Gamble is adept in its early discussions with technology partners not to ask for confidential disclosures. Instead it creates carefully crafted questionnaires for technology partners to answer specific questions about whether their solutions can deliver certain performance and benefit outcomes. Only when P&G is satisfied with these answers does it pursue confidential information for deeper due diligence.

- In our work for the Weight Management Collaborative mentioned above, the teaming agreements we developed for GSK, Microsoft, Kraft, Rodale, and others ensured that each company's existing I/P was protected and any improvement opportunities developed from consumer interaction and engagement with startups were predetermined to be licensed back via royalty-free rights in perpetuity for their own fields of use.

- In both the Weight Management Collaborative and Third Screen Marketplace consortia that I've mentioned, the participating large companies were coached and trained in how to conduct initial engagement sessions with startups, ensuring a focus on learning about capabilities and opportunities and avoiding brainstorming or ideation when the only agreements in place were the nondisclosure type.

Based on the experience of other companies and my own in managing I/P issues with clients, here's a stepwise approach that you can consider for your own engagements:

1. Begin with nonconfidential discussions, with written agreement upfront not to disclose confidential information.

2. As confidence in an opportunity increases, proceed to nondisclosure agreements for initial discussions and diligence; always remind partners at this point to simply explore, not co-invent.

3. Then move to teaming agreements that enable external exploration in the market and with customers; address existing I/P and sharing of limited new I/P creation in these agreements.

4. Finally, move to more in-depth co-development and option agreements that spell out roles and responsibilities and complete intellectual property rights for co-development in detail, but only once the companies have progressed through simpler levels of collaboration.

Dondeena Bradley (Weight Watchers) summed it up well when she told me, "If corporations have cultures that are too controlling, they hinder innovation and breakthroughs. I honestly believe that with the cost of maintaining patents and the speed of business today, we need to embrace a new openness. Companies need to move from a mindset of 'What can we own and protect?' to 'Where are the places that we can learn and experiment?' Sometimes being a feeder or teacher to the entrepreneur or a partner helps to bring good ideas forward rather than holding tight to them."

THE ROLE OF CONTENTION: IT'S A GOOD THING

Creating the future isn't always fun and games. One thing I counsel clients and venture partners to remember is this: don't be afraid to fight (a little). When dealing with collaborative innovation and venturing, the larger goal is not just about finding ideas but also about partnering with others to co-develop them. Sometimes, as is the case when more than one human being has an idea and a goal, this is an area where conflict can arise. Ideas + creativity + driven people = you get the idea.

But before you lament contention and disagreement, I am here to tell you that these things are not just inevitable but also powerful and productive parts of the process.

Contention tests your assumptions, sometimes vigorously. When everyone is getting along well, sometimes problems are hidden or swept under the rug. This may be more pleasant, but it doesn't help the process. Stan Lech, previously VP of innovation at GSK Consumer Healthcare, puts it this way: "Corporate cultures and the bad economy have really prevented people from having a voice, from taking chances, because people feel that they have to be collegial, they have to be overly collaborative, have to be agreeable. They don't want to be on the wrong side, because they're afraid of losing their job."

Resolving problems before milestones may be uncomfortable, but this benefits the team and the project at the end of the day. A launch is about more than looking good to the project manager(s) or senior management. To be resolved—and they will need to be sooner or later—issues need to be out in the open and on the table.

In managing Mobile Futures, Ed Kaczmarek understood the importance of addressing the issue head-on. He told me, "If any issues came up, as legal did, we would dive right into them and deal with them. We said to everyone, this is all about intense collaboration. If you see something going on that you don't like, or this, or that, just raise your hand and let's talk about it right away and solve it. It wasn't about letting something fester for two or three weeks, and then someone develops resentment, and then suddenly they're not doing anything together. That really worked."

Contention needs to be allowed and explored. Some amount of creative tension is a good thing. Openness and honesty are necessary for getting issues on the table and eventually resolved, for a long-term productive relationship.

DEFINING FUTURE BUSINESSES WITH LOWE'S

Lowe's Innovation Labs provides a compelling example of co-creating new opportunities in new emerging areas. The company is exploring a wide range of opportunities and some very innovative new technology-driven concepts. One of the first prototypes revealed by Kyle Nel and his team is the Holoroom, which uses 3D technology and augmented reality to allow users to take a virtual walk through a room with the fixtures and coverings they've designed. Lowe's defines these opportunities such as the Holoroom very quickly through co-created working prototypes within the company's physical incubators.

KYLE NEL,
EXECUTIVE DIRECTOR, LOWE'S INNOVATION LABS

Kyle Nel has an unusual approach to defining breakthrough opportunities: science-fiction narratives. Nel explains how Lowe's Innovation Labs is bringing together uncommon partners to imagine, define, and then build future breakthroughs for Lowe's and its consumers.

Corporations are very good at incrementally improving the things they did to become a corporation. Business is not a linear thing. You can't continually improve on your one thing and expect to be in business for the long haul. Brands you can name such as Circuit City and others that aren't around anymore didn't take that into account. More importantly, they didn't take action.

Because changes are happening faster and occurring in more divergent and harder to predict ways, it's very hard to have a defensive strategy. It's hard to know what to acquire or know what systems to build that will keep your platform going.

We decided to try to capitalize on this exponential world by getting ahead of it. The way that we do that at Lowe's Innovation Labs is founded on something called science-fiction prototyping.

Basically, you give all of your marketing research, your trend data, and other things to professional, published science-fiction writers. You give them a dossier of sorts on everything that's in there. You go through structured sessions with them, and then they write stories about how these trends and technologies will influence people's behavior in certain time horizons, like two, five, and 10 years down the road.

Science predicted the car, but science fiction predicted the traffic jam. I'm interested in the problems and the possible opportunities that are going to arrive from trends and technology coming together.

To be able to present the story in comic book form showing how these trends could change people's behavior, especially our customers' behavior, is pretty powerful. It's an actual story with characters and conflict and resolution; like a real story, everyone can build on it in his or her own way. I've never seen a tool, strategic or otherwise, where people, at all levels inside the organization, really build on it in a meaningful way. The narrative really helps.

Take, for instance, the Holoroom. It seems obvious now, but three years ago when we wrote the story, Oculus Rift didn't exist, or at least most hadn't heard about it. The things that are now so obvious, they weren't really around.

The goal is to make things that don't exist anywhere else and bring them into the Lowe's ecosystem on a test basis to try out and see whether there's anything there. That's how I feel we'll be able to push innovation forward—by quickly showing the value of the storytelling and how fast you can really effect change in the marketplace and inside the company as well.

Then we move very quickly to working prototypes. We want to put them in people's hands sooner rather than later. I'd rather put something out there in the market at least in a small test that's not 100% perfect but works so we can learn quickly, adapt, and iterate.

We want to create things that don't exist, and we work with a variety of partners to bring them to life. Startups are very skeptical of corporates that say that they want to partner or want to work together. They can smell it if the person on the corporate side doesn't really fully understand what he or she is talking about.

For us, part of the solution is to have these labs where we can say to the startups, "I'd love to invite you down in two weeks to work with our team, and we'll show you at least the basic idea of what we're working on. We can prove it out together to really make sure that you can do what you say you can do and then vice versa. We can show you that we're very serious about what you're doing, and we can also show you how we might incorporate what you're working on into something larger."

Having that lab space, we can bring people in and really build those relationships and then show that we both know where we're going with this technology. A lot of the other corporate labs that I've seen are really not so big on the co-creation as much as they are on the acquisition.

That's a misstep. Not that there's anything wrong with acquisition, but co-creation is extremely powerful.

There are large parts of the Holoroom that didn't exist, and we had to co-create it with those partners to be able to make this thing work. I just think it's so powerful, but it is messy. You have to have a commitment from your larger organization to be able to work through those messy parts.

Working closely with the Lowe's organization is also critical. You can have the most amazing tool, but if it's not integrated into the company's strategy, it might as well not even exist.

What overall advice would I give? I would say that there's an inherent risk in standing still or just focusing on incremental improvement. The other part of that is if people, even inside of your organization, aren't openly mocking you or giggling when you bring up where you want to go, you probably aren't pushing it far enough.

This is an amazing time to be working for a large organization where you can really effect change and you can change the lives of millions of people. It's an exciting time to be able to work on disruptive innovation in a large company like Lowe's that's taken a chance on me and on the labs to be able to do these kinds of things. Everybody in our space should just be so happy to work on this stuff. It's incredible.

Kyle Nel is the executive director of Lowe's Innovation Labs, where he and his team are on the forefront of bringing together uncommon partners to imagine the impossible and co-create solutions that deliver new experiences for consumers through technology. Prior to Lowe's, Nel was part of Walmart's Global Insights group, where he contributed to shopper insights and innovation.

BUSINESS MODEL INNOVATION

Defining opportunities in and of itself involves iteration and experimentation. Disruptions are often thought of as technology breakthroughs. But business model innovation is often the real opportunity, and it may or may not involve technology. Even with a technology breakthrough, the important focus still needs to be on how best to monetize it.

So, what is business model innovation? It's a powerful way to move beyond simple product or service innovation and leverage how you go to market, how you generate revenue, and how you structure a venture to create new value. New business creation is exploratory and iterative. Don't fall into the trap of innovating just the product or service. Entrepreneurship involves exploring innovation in every aspect of the business.

Steve Blank has said, "Existing companies execute a business model. Startups search for one." To help you with exploring and testing a variety of business models, I'll introduce a business model mapping framework that ensures that alternative business models are creatively explored and well defined.

THE BUSINESS MODEL CONCEPT MAP

In my firm, Venture2, we have an approach we use in our own ventures and with our clients called new venture jumpstarts that focuses on quickly exploring a variety of unique approaches to the venture and the business model. It's designed to bring some balance of right-brain/left-brain thinking to corporate business planning, where today we often see an overabundance of left-brain thinking.

One of the key tools we use is the business model concept map that we developed as a hybrid of some well-established frameworks in the market. Our framework is an evolution of a well-accepted tool called a strategy table, which helps to identify key strategic levers and provides a way to put together new combinations to create alternative strategies. We've applied this to business modeling, and we've been evolving and improving our approach for years. I'll share just the basic approach here.

You may have heard of the business model canvas, a tool for business model exploration that was initially developed by Alexander Osterwalder. I think this is a great framework and one that has done much to bring business model generation to the forefront in new venture development.

While this tool is certainly very useful, we've felt at my firm that a framework that can help drive more options and ensure integration of these options can also assist teams in pushing their thinking and creating even better solutions. So if you're using the canvas or other approaches, great. Decide for yourself what tools and approaches work best for your teams and situations.

CREATING BUSINESS MODEL CONCEPT MAPS

First, the process works best when it's a cross-functional activity, with representatives from marketing, technical, finance, and other relevant areas. Don't think it needs to be only an internal corporate exercise. I've used it with peer-to-peer collaborations between established companies and in co-ventures between large companies and entrepreneurial firms.

Step 0: Before beginning the business model mapping effort, do the upfront work to ensure that the venture has a clearly defined vision, including some measures of success, constraints, and the needs of each party.

Step 1: Identify the strategic levers relevant to the venture at hand. Strategic levers are the variables at your disposal for bringing a big idea to market. These comprise the columns of the framework. We start with a predefined set of levers, but that's only a starting point. You have the flexibility to substitute what makes sense for your situation.

The levers we propose as a starting point are:

- Customer target
- Customer problem
- Value proposition
- Offering(s)

- Revenue model(s)
- Cost model(s)
- Distribution
- Partnering approach

I'll define these in a bit more detail below and use a disguised example to bring the strategic levers to life in the chart that follows.

Step 2: For the strategic levers, identify a realistic menu of options for each that the venture could potentially explore or pursue. You'll likely add to this menu as you begin to develop strategy options and additional choices for some strategic levers become evident.

Step 3: Map the default strategy. This may not always be true, but, generally, the team has a going-in assumption about most of the elements of the business model. Document it right upfront. It's a healthy exercise, and it gives you a comparator as you explore new options.

Step 4: Now comes the fun part: basically a mixing-and-matching exercise to force teams to get beyond the obvious and explore new options. Pick a column. As an example, let's say customer problem. Because you would have (hopefully) already done customer development work, the choices now for customer problem are likely variations on a well-defined general target. For each "menu" choice under that column, use that item as the stake in the ground for that strategy option. Then the group should develop one or more strategies that are choices from the other columns—with one important caveat: for each strategic option you develop, the choices from the other columns shouldn't be random but rather a logical and coherent set of choices that together comprise that option.

Step 5: Iterate on the process above. In our experience, we'll have multiple breakout subgroups each pick a column and use that as their basis for building options across all strategic levers. You'll be surprised and amazed at the creative (and yet internally coherent) strategies that emerge. Like any creative exercise, start broad and fast and then go back, deselect the options that don't pass the commonsense test, and do it again by combining and refining some of the more promising options surfaced.

Step 6: Develop business model summary statements for the most promising of the options surfaced. Each should be documented on a slide or simple one-page graphic summary. Again, do what's appropriate for you, but we like to have the following as core elements of each strategy summary:

- Description of the strategy (target, offerings, etc.)

- Rationale

- Rough financial estimates (size of prize)

- Risks/uncertainties

Step 7: Design experiments to test hypotheses. Define specific learning objectives that can reduce risk and then conduct limited-scope experiments to test your hypotheses around customer need, product/market fit, partnering approach, and related objectives.

Iterate on the above until you have a promising direction that is worth moving to the next phase of development. In the above steps you may have done this as a corporate team or perhaps with the entrepreneurial team being explored for partnership.

BUSINESS MODEL CONCEPT MAPS IN ACTION

In this generic example of business model mapping (Fig. 7.1), you can see how each column has been developed with a number of options relevant to a particular opportunity. The selections circled represent a business model option and are but one of a wide variety of possible combinations across these strategic levers. Remember that each of these business model options is not created by randomly selecting from each column; rather, no matter which column you start with, select only choices from the other columns that comprise a logical and coherent strategy. There are many.

Looking at this graphic, you can get a better sense of how the strategic levers I discussed come into play.

BUSINESS MODEL CONCEPT MAP - EXAMPLE

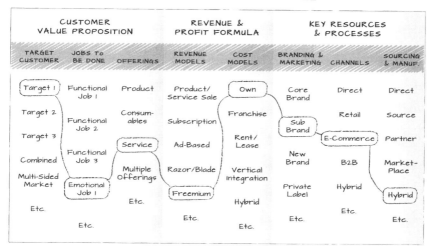

FIG. 7.1

Now let's try another. Imagine this scenario for a new venture idea.

Opportunity Statement: "Genie," Your Personal Travel Concierge: personalized, on-demand concierge service and app for the frequent business traveler

Validated Target Customer: Frequent business travelers working for themselves or small companies, who fly more than 50K miles and stay more than 30 hotel nights per year (US focus initially)

Validated Customer Problem: Unforeseen travel problems are a large source of stress for these travelers.

Because the target customer and problem are validated already in this example, we'll start with these and select coherent options from the other columns (Fig. 7.2). Note that, for example, under offerings we're not compelled to choose only one.

GENIE TRAVEL CONCIERGE

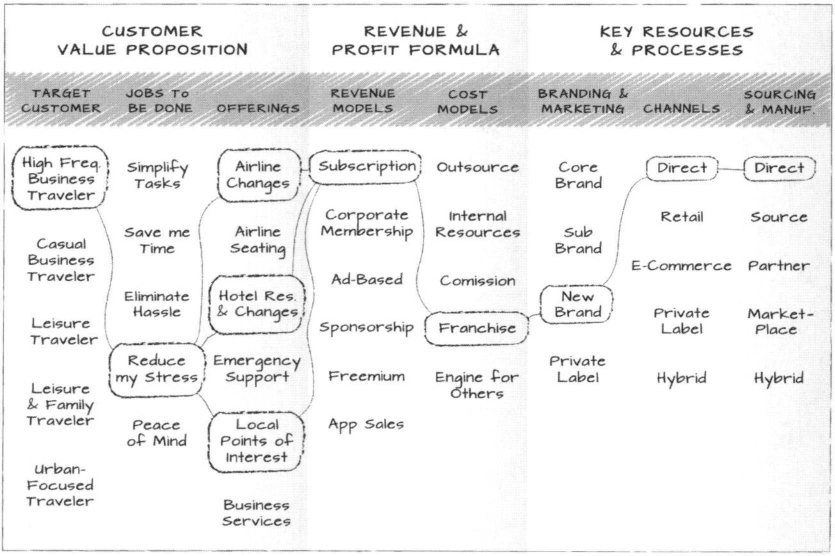

FIG. 7.2

We can create an almost endless number of options from this process. The key is to use the tool to ensure divergent thinking and create nonobvious solutions but then to hone in on the business models and approaches that make sense for the team to develop further. In a typical workshop we'll create 10–15 strategic options and then prioritize and refine the more attractive ones. Often this will then surface even better options by combining some of the best elements of each. This process has been very successful in helping teams break through to nonobvious business models that can be a source of differentiation. Ultimately, this is still just an exercise, and the real learning comes from testing and validating these business models with customers and in-market experiments.

WHIRLPOOL DEFINES A NEW BUSINESS MODEL

Back in 2004, Whirlpool developed an innovative new home "appliance" called the Personal Valet, which was, in essence, a home dry-cleaning device. Consumer research showed high interest, Whirlpool saw an opportunity to create a whole new category of appliances, and the business model allowed for recurring revenue via the solutions that were part of the system. Sounds like a winner. Whirlpool developed a first-generation product yet was still not confident of the market demand for such a high-risk product, and so it chose Abt Electronics, a well-known "destination" housewares retailer, for its only rollout in this single (sprawling) store. While Whirlpool could have applied more lean thinking earlier in development (as what it tooled up was definitely not an MVP), it did have the foresight to conduct this in-market experiment for a soft launch before committing the tens of millions of dollars needed for a national marketing campaign and the massive inventory needed to fill the pipeline of its existing broad retailer network. The result? It bombed. Completely. Maybe the economics of home dry cleaning made sense, but the convenience of dropping off these items without a hassle was too high a switching cost to overcome. So, while the product was a failure, Whirlpool's in-market experiment saved the company tens of millions of dollars and, importantly, time and resources.

Here's an update to that story, 10 years later. P&G and Whirlpool announced in mid-2014 the Swash system for home fabric care, which combines a Whirlpool durable and a P&G consumable (I'm guessing it's Febreze derived). The consumer proposition is very similar to the Personal Valet, and the device will retail for $499. It does promise a faster time and lower price and is significantly more portable than the previous iteration. Whirlpool is partnering with P&G in creating this new business model, but P&G was also the consumables partner in the Personal Valet project in 2004. Interestingly, Whirlpool initially tested distribution via a single retail partner again, this time at Bloomingdales. With that success, Whirlpool and P&G have expanded Swash distribution and are now applying their collective marketing expertise to hopefully creating a new consumer category. They are targeting a specific consumer need for freshening clothing and not trying to completely replace trips to the dry cleaner. Time will tell if the new business can scale, but I give them credit for continuing to experiment with new business models and breakthrough products. Whirlpool is putting an increasing focus on new business creation and we can expect to see more from them in the coming years.

TRUST AS A MOMENTUM BUILDER

The approaches I'm outlining in this chapter are aimed at getting your teams focused on external opportunities, as well as the consumer and the market, before getting mired in the messy and sometimes overly complicated negotiations of a specific deal. I'll speak more about these dynamics in chapter 9, where the focus is integration. In the meantime, I'd like to outline another benefit of this collective approach to defining opportunities.

If you can find a way to create and encourage engagement—especially externally focused engagement—prior to formal development agreements, you'll begin the critical process of building trust much sooner in the process. Co-creation, especially in creating new businesses together, is as much about trust and relationships as it is about strategy and execution. I was amazed to see in our speed-dating events how, with just a little bit of interaction, trust was quickly built and many preconceived notions fell away. In these sessions, it was almost funny to see time and time again how the entrepreneurs would start to open up about their "better ideas" that they'd been afraid to discuss once they were able to sit across the table from an executive instead of picturing the company as a faceless behemoth. The sooner you can create a personal relationship, the faster you both can move on to the more profitable business kind.

8

INCUBATE: EVOLVE
AND ACCELERATE

INCUBATE

3

Ideas are a dime a dozen. The challenge is nurturing and evolving them into marketable innovations and sustainable businesses. In new business creation (vs. new product or service development), the risks and unknowns are even higher. So, our ability to incubate new business opportunities and demonstrate market viability to justify scale-up is critically important.

This chapter is focused on helping you structure and manage the incubation phase and presents examples from leading companies that are finding creative ways to engage with entrepreneurs and startups in doing so. We'll discuss some approaches and detail the key steps any enterprise must take to ensure that great new business ideas are nurtured and evolved in market.

THE CHALLENGE OF CORPORATE INCUBATION

The marketplace is littered with stories of established companies attempting breakthrough opportunities via new types of partnerships and incubation models:

- In 2006, Home Depot announced, with great fanfare, the launch of Orange Works, an innovation lab in partnership with Arnell Group (at the time a leading design and ad agency). The company launched an initial flurry of product innovations, but the initiative died quickly when Home Depot hit economic challenges.

- In its prime during the period of 2000–2008, Nokia Innovent was a hybrid corporate venture capital and incubator activity within Nokia that was very active in both investing and nurturing externally sourced innovations for mobile. Innovent's mission was based on collaboration and company building for Nokia. Even prior to the sale of Nokia to Microsoft, Innovent's demise was sealed when senior management shifted focus to the company's turnaround and deemphasized new business creation.

- Qualcomm Venture Fest began in 2006 and evolved into a contest-driven new venture process with internal teams that were supplemented by external technologies and ideas. The process was successful in surfacing not only product ideas but also new business models such as Zeebo, a low-cost game console for developing countries. Eventually, to quell internal friction between Venture Fest and the core R&D groups, R&D absorbed Venture Fest in 2011 and it has evolved into a series of innovation challenges.

I would not characterize these examples as failures but rather as experiments in the ongoing search for the right models to drive successful new business incubation and creation. Target, Walmart, Microsoft, Nike, P&G, Samsung, and many other large companies have launched their own corporate incubators and placed these units in Silicon Valley and other global innovation hot spots. Johnson & Johnson's innovation centers are an interesting hybrid model in which J&J and startup teams engage more deeply through co-working, incubation, and investment.

Microsoft, Nike, and now Disney have gone the route of partnering with an established accelerator (in this case Techstars, a top accelerator). Accelerators such as Techstars review thousands of prospects each year and then admit a small cohort during a defined period where they're accelerated with a limited amount of capital and infused with world-class mentorship from a network of proven entrepreneurs. Each graduating class is then presented to its network of VCs for potential investment. What's new is the increasing number of corporations engaging with these accelerators with hopes of infusing some entrepreneurial thinking and technologies to support their growth and innovation agenda.

In a 2014 study conducted by the Boston Consulting Group across six industries, 43% of the top 10 companies in each industry (defined by market value) have established incubators or accelerators—this compared with 23% of the top 30 companies in each industry. Geographic hot spots such as Silicon Valley, London, and Tel Aviv are popular locations, under the premise that getting plugged into the flow of ideas will accelerate innovation. There's truth to that, but it's not a panacea, either. Dave Knox (Rockfish/the Brandery) said to me, "I think if you're doing it to get a headline in the press, that's probably the wrong reason to do it. Saying you've planted your flag and you're open for business, I don't think anybody really cares about that. It's got to be the right intentions for why you're getting involved with that community. Silicon Valley is a place of great inspiration, but it's also not the sole source of innovation in our country."

As these experiments and others play out, the models will continue to evolve as large companies search for the right formula for getting in on the disruption game.

What can we learn from some of the experiments so far?

First, senior-level corporate visibility and support are keys to success. Establishing and building a venture are daunting tasks. I know. You're trying to build support for your vision and demonstrate that the big idea you believe in so much is investable. To do that you're remortgaging your home, forgoing sleep, and trying to stay resilient in the face of a never-ending gauntlet of failures and disappointment. But that perseverance is a critical ingredient for success. So, in the case of corporate venturing, now you're facing challenges not only from the outside world but also from the corporate anti-bodies who see this approach as a threat to their own security and jobs. You're looking for strong and visible support from senior leaders who normally measure everything by a P&L and quarterly returns, and you're asking them to believe in your dream, to withhold judging it by the traditional measures, and to place a bet on a high-risk, high-return opportunity.

Second, a degree of autonomy and separation from the mother ship is required for incubation of new ventures. I first mentioned in chapter 4 the analogy of creating "an island with a bridge to the mainland." Separation is important in physical, organizational, and management approaches in the incubation phase. Not surprisingly, Nike's Nike+ Fuel Lab has been located near its headquarters but a few miles away, tucked away from the day-to-day oversight and politics of the core business. So, while separation is important, some degree of connection remains important, especially ensuring visibility with senior management, who must provide air cover for incubators and venture creation teams. Remember polarity thinking? Autonomy and integration are another set of polarities that should be leveraged and managed, and we need elements of both. Ultimately, these new businesses will need to be integrated into the organization if they can scale. We'll discuss this integration in more detail in chapter 9.

Third, the incentives and reward systems of new business incubation and creation will need to be different from those of the core business units. The culture and reward systems of large companies do not lend themselves to nurturing risky new business ventures. The leaders and teams (whether corporate led or entrepreneur led) engaged in incubating these businesses need to be measured and rewarded both on their ability to de-risk big ideas and with the carrot of shared rewards should the venture succeed. And rewards are not only financial—recognition and control over one's own work and other forms of rewards are important to passionate innovation teams as well.

THREE MODELS FOR BUSINESS INCUBATION

We'll never see a one-size-fits-all solution for corporate ventures or business incubation teams. Here are three ways to look at structuring your incubation efforts that address the success factors I've highlighted.

INSIDE-IN (Integrated)

This model assumes that ventures can be incubated within the core business structure while engaging external partners. It's a model that's difficult to manage internally for disruptive opportunities and often comes down to the innovation maturity of the organization.

Within this model is a spectrum of options, from *dedicated* internal groups to completely *distributed* models where new business incubation is managed directly within the business units. Very few companies in the world can manage the distributed model, where disruption is everyone's job, for all the reasons I've laid out in this book. 3M is a pretty unique example, with innovation being so ingrained in the DNA of the company. I'm there each year for an innovation conference, and it's an inspiring company in many ways. I wouldn't recommend distributed models for most. Even leaders such as P&G, Jarden, and Qualcomm have set up dedicated business creation units. The history of corporate business creation shows a challenging road as well. P&G eliminated its FutureWorks team but has maintained a dedicated group focused on new business creation. Unilever, until recently, had a dedicated new business unit but has moved those responsibilities to the Unilever Ventures group (where it will likely be more focused on acquisition than incubation).

Visibility and Support: The inside-in model of venture incubation provides a challenging path, and so visibility and support are important. Being internal, visibility should be better. It's lower risk for the organization but can be harder to ensure senior management air cover, due to the distributed nature of the initiatives.

Autonomy: Autonomy is also generally low, as it's the most integrated within the existing structure. It becomes very difficult to justify different operating norms and measures for an internal group sharing facilities and infrastructure with the business units, but it can be done.

Incentives: Finally, the incentives are usually not conducive to entrepreneurial ventures because structuring shared risk/reward models from within the existing business structure is nearly impossible. Still, it can be done, and in the future as new business creation efforts become more widespread and organizations more attuned to co-venturing, this inside-in model becomes more viable.

Qualcomm's Venture Fest fits the inside-in model in that Ricardo dos Santos (who led these efforts) built the program primarily around sourcing both inside and outside ideas and then put together venture teams for each of the more promising ideas and gave these employees an opportunity to experience working in a more entrepreneurial structure and speed.

IBM has been managing its Emerging Business Opportunities (EBO) group since 2000 and has delivered $26 billion in incremental revenue for IBM since it was created. IBM, historically challenged with starting new businesses in spite of having many new ideas, created the EBO program to incubate and then scale internal startups that leveraged ideas from inside and out (e.g., customers and venture capital firms). These emerging businesses have a strong, experienced leader and benefit from senior-level sponsorship, dedicated resources, and limited autonomy (to protect it from corporate anti-bodies) and balance this with direct linkages to the business units to ensure that EBOs are addressing strategic needs. One of the first EBO wins within IBM was a wireless technology venture to bring the technology into automotive and other nontraditional applications, achieving $2.4 billion in sales in its third year.

P&G's Align brand provides another strong example of an entrepreneurial incubation and launch of this fledgling business within a larger structure of P&G.

The strategy P&G employed is one it had used before on other products, notably, Swiffer. This "diffusion marketing" process is one that builds the business in slow motion, a one-step-at-a-time pace. The early rollout of Align, P&G's daily probiotic supplement, focused on online communities of specific digestive disorder sufferers as well as physicians. At first, the product was sold only online and via telephone. In 2008, Align expanded to retail distribution in three markets, Cincinnati, Dallas, and St. Louis, with specific retail partners, including Walgreens, CVS, Walmart, and Meijer. Finally, Align was launched nationally. Sales increased steadily in 2010 and 2011. In 2010 the product won the Edison Best New Product in the Consumer Packaged Goods, Consumer Drug Segment, Category. In mid-2012, it won a Nielsen Breakthrough Silver Innovation.

What worked for P&G? The stair-step rollout and a dedicated cross-functional business team running this business as a venture. At each step of the launch, the company was able to prove viability and muster support to move on.

The behind-the-scenes story is that the strategy was one of necessity. With an unproven market and a lot of potential risks and barriers to the adoption of Align, particularly around the unknowable issue of consumer compliance, this initiative's odds of getting to P&G-level scalable clearly were not that high. As was relayed to me by one of the initial leaders of the effort, this team took it upon themselves to try a simple web strategy out of desperation. Nothing more entrepreneurial than a team with no resources and the odds stacked against them but a belief in a business opportunity. The rest is history.

INSIDE-OUT (Accelerator Models)

Dedicated corporate accelerators and corporate tie-ins to existing startup accelerators are a hot trend today, evidenced by the BCG study. One

advantage of the inside-out model is that it accomplishes the goal of creating separation and autonomy for venture teams to incubate new businesses. It also lends itself naturally to co-creation that involves startups that already thrive in these types of incubators. As mentioned, Techstars partnered with both Microsoft and Nike+ to set up and run their corporate incubators. The model that Techstars and its corporate partners use is the traditional accelerator model of recruiting a cohort of startups (in this case, aligned with the goals of the corporate partner) and providing financial and expert mentoring support in addition to direct interaction with representatives from the corporation. The accelerator model works well in creating an efficient and simple business model but does little to promote deeper co-creation beyond a typical 120-day incubation program.

Visibility and Support: In general, the inside-out model of venture incubation requires strong senior management support to even be launched, but maintaining that support can be difficult with physical separation.

Autonomy: While separation and autonomy are high, the linkages to the corporation are generally weak, and senior management visibility is a key risk for both eventual integration and support.

Incentives: This structure can more easily be customized for properly incentivizing venturing teams because it most closely resembles the traditional startup culture and financial rewards.

We discussed in chapter 6 the P&G example of imbedding an executive in Shopkick to guide the company and better ensure that it considered brand needs (and not just retailer needs). This is one example of the inside-out model.

Samsung has a dedicated accelerator, and it too is set up to ensure separation from the core business—a lot of separation, being in Silicon Valley, many thousands of miles away from headquarters in South Korea. David Eun (the EVP who leads it) does a great job of advocating for the effort and regularly receives entourages of Samsung executives to show-case their efforts and expose leadership to Silicon Valley. One unique aspect of Samsung's model is that it actually acquires its startups prior to entering the accelerator. No question on alignment there. This makes it harder to find truly big ideas when seed-stage or even idea-stage founders rarely want to sell out their equity so soon. But for the entrepreneur who wants more security, this model works, and for Samsung, its ability to find gems among the many seed-stage companies struggling for funding creates a buyer's market.

Lowe's Innovation Labs, which was presented in chapter 7, is another example of a corporate accelerator. In this case, it's less about accelerat-ing a large number of startups and more of a true laboratory for Lowe's own programs where it can bring in entrepreneurs and other external partners on a targeted basis. Kyle Nel of Lowe's emphasized to me the importance of its physical space as well. He said, "What I've learned time and time again is that building strong relationships and bringing those people together in a physical space at least some part of the time is critical to moving things forward fast."

Coca-Cola has been expanding a very interesting corporate accelerator program of its own called the Coca-Cola Founders Platform. David Butler, Coca-Cola's VP of innovation and entrepreneurship, has shared through numerous forums his belief that all parties win when startups move to scale-ups. That's why Coca-Cola has taken a unique approach by focus-ing on co-creating *with* startups and making its assets available to proven cofounders and then bringing Coke's amazing ability to scale. By recruit-ing external founders and then letting them build new companies around Coca-Cola's assets, relationships, and resources, Coca-Cola gets early access to new opportunities, and the founders gain an unfair advantage through their relationship with this leading brand company. Entrepreneurs have been recruited in eight global locations and then matched with local Coca-Cola regional teams to pursue a variety of digital and service innovations. Wonolo is one of these co-created startups. It's focused on providing on-demand staffing for hourly/daily jobs, such as retail shelf restocking. Coca-Cola is creating a whole new approach to inside-out that can leverage the best of the enterprise and the entrepreneur.

In June of 2014, GE announced a partnership with Frost Data Capital in launching Frost I3, an incubator for the industrial Internet. This is yet another twist on the model of inside-out: in this case, GE is partnering with an up-and-coming venture capital firm that specializes in big-data startups. The model is built on applying lean methodology in nurturing these startups. Frost brings capital and methodology, while GE brings deep expertise in areas such as predictive analytics and intelligent machinery. Hence both organizations are recruiting and supporting startups, and the startups have the potential for a great exit via GE. Frost Data Capital's investment strategy is one of incubation and then quick exit, so the model makes sense for both organizations, and the narrow scope enables more focused scouting and clear messaging in outreach.

Inside-out takes many forms, but all are aimed at leveraging the entrepreneurial ecosystem more directly in the incubation process to achieve corporate growth goals.

OUTSIDE-IN (Imbedded Entrepreneurs)

Another model for collaboration is to imbed external partners and entrepreneurs into corporate ventures. It's more difficult to pull off, especially if you don't have the right entrepreneurs who can navigate the corporate  landscape and avoid the landmines. However, with the right people, corporate teams that might normally be stuck or fall prey to politics and meddling can engage external Sherpas who can challenge norms and infuse entrepreneurial thinking into the organization.

Visibility and Support: The outside-in model of venture incubation provides an easier approach to gain and retain senior management visibility and support.

Autonomy: While autonomy is low with this model, it can work if the initiative is managed somewhat outside of the core business structure, as it is with Jarden (Transformational Innovation reports directly to the senior leadership team).

Incentives: Within a corporate environment, creating big wins for an entrepreneur is difficult, but there are ways to ensure that incentives are supportive of entrepreneurial success. Often, the draw for the entrepreneur is the ability to work with a team and on a platform that can have a big impact. Incentives aren't always about money.

A classic example that we'll cover in more detail in chapter 9 comes from P&G and the Crest Spinbrush. In this program, two external entrepreneurs from Dr. John's (a company that licensed its spin brush to P&G) were imbedded inside P&G during the development and transition to scale up this business, which became a phenomenal success for both P&G and the entrepreneurs.

AthenaHealth has created an interesting model called the MDP Accelerator (MDP stands for More Disruption Please). Its onsite accelerator is searching for and incubating early-stage startups that the company believes can disrupt healthcare. AthenaHealth is a practice management and EMR (electronic medical records) provider, so it has deep and broad access to healthcare providers, which it can leverage to support these startups. It offers 8–12 months of residence to the startups and mentoring from the AthenaHealth team, as well as from its network of healthcare providers. The first successfully launched startup, Smart Scheduling, is focused on eliminating the inefficiencies of patient scheduling and no-shows for healthcare providers.

Another recent example of outside-in comes from Jarden Consumer Solutions and the launch of its Crock-Pot Cuisine line of gourmet foods. Jarden's Transformational Innovation (TI) group, charged with disruptive new business creation, managed this venture.

In this case, Jarden is committed to getting beyond selling durable products and creating recurring revenue streams and more consumer interactions with a brand that is highly regarded and trusted, Crock-Pot. Aside from the uniqueness of the business model, what's impressive about Jarden's approach is that it recognized that successfully launching this venture required skills the internal team didn't have. So what did Jarden do? It recruited a proven entrepreneur with deep experience in both the food category and direct-to-consumer models to help lead the initiative.

Bryan Janeczko, a New York City–based entrepreneur, had launched Nu-Kitchen, a fresh meals–to–home subscription model that dealt with many of the challenges JCS now faced, ranging from web-based ordering systems and order fulfillment to building a consumer base. Janeczko successfully sold his business to Nutrisystem, so he clearly understands how to position a new direct-to-consumer food business to be scaled. Rather than hire him directly (as both parties knew the fit would not be long term), Jarden structured a defined period, put in place incentives beyond contracting fees, and enabled this entrepreneur to guide the initiative from within Jarden Consumer Solutions. The business is now out of beta, and early indications are that the business is a winning one and scalable too. Just as importantly, Jarden has demonstrated the insourcing of entrepreneurial talent and the commercializing of a very different business model for the company's future.

BRYAN JANECZKO,
FOUNDER, WICKED START

Where is the meeting point between corporate and startup in the new business incubation process? Bryan Janeczko sees that juncture and looks for ways to make it work for both parties.

The difference between a corporate entrepreneur and a startup entrepreneur is that a corporate entrepreneur usually has not created a business startup himself or herself. The mindset is really the big difference. It's about your tolerance for risk. What is your tolerance for being able to confront challenges and to be flexible? At the end of the day, someone's going to ask you, "How flexible are you? How quick? How adaptable are you? Are you able to work in a really diverse environment of ups and downs?" You might say, "Yes. Yes. Yes." However, fundamentally, it comes back to the passion for whatever it is you're developing.

The ability to creatively problem solve—that's really what this is about. Once you've defined what it is that you're solving for, the whitespace or the opportunity, then you have to layer on benchmarks for success. If we're going to pursue this, what are some of the KPIs that we want to look to measure? What is possible in the short term versus the long term? We're incubating this from concept to commercialization. That's where you need to marry startup methodologies with the corporate infrastructure.

A company might recognize that by investing $1 or $2 million into a particular initiative, and that if there was a high probability of success, it could increase overall revenues by $10, $20, $30 million. If there's a 50% chance of increasing revenues that much within five years, it sounds like it's a good investment. However, you don't want to put the same quarterly KPIs in place that you would for a normal business. Instead of saying, "We're going to give you X this quarter and we want to see Y results," if you don't see it, well, can we explain why or make the needed adjustments? If so, then we'll invest for the next quarter. It's the same process. We need to shift that mindset when creating new businesses. You can't think of a startup as a mini corporate entity. If you do, you'll fail. My role is often to help educate corporate folks and bring them along for that journey.

I've been an external entrepreneur working in a corporate environment. If you're an external entrepreneur, you tend to be not as rigorous in terms of the hierarchy, in terms of process, in terms of organizational structure—which can work for and against you. It's great if you're coming up with ideas and you're trying to brainstorm and think of an opportunity that you might want to develop, but in terms of getting the structure and process in place to create a scalable business, that often is where many early-stage entrepreneurs are lacking.

An entrepreneur may come in to help identify or develop an idea initially, but then you bring in the MBAs to implement the structure and process. It's those processes that are going to create scalability and growth in the long term. I don't know of a single successful firm, technology or otherwise, that's really been able to grow and scale without having an infrastructure put in place once the concept has gained traction. Even Facebook. If it weren't for the initial investors who brought seasoned professionals to the table, that business might not be where it is. It's straightforward. You need both.

Bryan Janeczko is the founder of Wicked Start, a venture advisory firm focusing on wellness and technology. He was previously codirector of the Founder Institute in New York City. Janeczko is a seasoned entrepreneur with multiple startups under his belt, including Nu-Kitchen, a consumer subscription-based meal service that was sold to Nutrisystem.

THE THREE MODELS OF INCUBATION ARE SITUATIONAL

The three models I've laid out above provide a useful framework for understanding how many other companies are experimenting with new approaches to business incubation. The models also constitute an instructive framework for considering your own approaches to incubation.

These models are not mutually exclusive and are more situational, so adapt them to suit your own needs. Incubation is about experimentation, and that includes the approach we use.

EXPERIMENT USING LEAN APPROACHES

Closely related to the concept of validated learning is building early versions of the product from the perspective of the absolute minimum needed versus the often traditional approach of providing many bells and whistles in the name of delivering additional value for the user/consumer. The minimum viable product (MVP) is a concept we discussed that comes from the lean movement and is the mechanism you can use in support of validated learning. I would also point you to a very closely related concept called pretotyping, conceived by Alberto Savoia at Google. Developed somewhat independently yet very analogous to the concept of the MVP, it's about making sure you are building the right "it" before you build "it" right—or, in Savoia's words, "faking it before you make it." Pretotyping, as documented in his book by the same name, is a growing movement of dedicated online communities and companies focused on promoting this practice.

Most of the young companies using lean principles are in the digital space, where MVPs are much easier to develop and launch in limited ways. In the context of incubation outside of software, the MVP concept is often lost or misunderstood. If you're developing a new drug or packaged good, the idea of MVP does not hold if taken as a literal concept. Instead, we help teams create elements of the business proposition that can be developed and tested, usually in market. Often, external partnerships enable additional ways to create/test MVPs.

So, by structuring experimentation as a series of learning experiments, the learning objectives of your particular stage of development are what will drive the MVP that you will need. This could be as simple as a pitch or a landing page you create, or it could be more of a concierge model to test the business model.

One of my favorite examples of incubating with a creative MVP comes from Robin Chase, cofounder of Zipcar. When she started her business, Chase bought a Volkswagen Beetle and added a very simple logo to the door. Then she placed an ad in her local Boston Craigslist to advertise availability of this new vehicle-sharing opportunity. When she received an inquiry by phone, she then provided the location of the vehicle (on a side street near her home) and instructed the renter to pick up the key under the bench cushion on her back porch. Truly an instructive and very valuable MVP if ever there was one!

Mike Rainone and his team at PCDworks are located on top of a mountain in east Texas. It's nearly a two-hour drive from Dallas, so be sure to watch out for the local speed trap as the speed limit drops outside of Athens, Texas. (They got me!) Once you finally get there, though, you'll have everything you need. Rainone and his team (which includes his wonderful wife, Donna, and daughter, Louise) host corporate teams interested in breakthrough technology development. Within the campus of offices and sleeping quarters, you'll also find electrical and mechanical engineering labs and a prototype shop with CNC machines, 3D printers, and other toys that most engineers would die for. Companies ranging from oil and gas clients to major food companies bring their teams for extended brainstorming sessions on new products and technologies and then can go right to the shop and build electromechanical prototypes of machines, products, and widgets faster than you can get your meeting minutes typed up if you're brainstorming at the home office.

I've worked with Rainone on many programs, and here's one example of that process. We were collaborating on a breakthrough idea for torque wrenches. Through end user interviews, we explored multiple segments and landed on an attractive and growing niche segment. We identified a unique opportunity to disrupt the consumer market for a specialized but rapidly growing segment of weekend-enthusiast mechanics. PCDworks was able to build rapid prototypes with the basic functionality of this technology that allowed us to go out and engage directly with users on what they liked and didn't like about each iteration. With feedback in hand, we could immediately build another nonfunctional "looks like" model and a functional (but ugly) "works like" prototype for additional user testing. We collapsed months or years of development into weeks. Following this work, the investors recruited an entrepreneur to lead a new business called Brownline Tools. PCDworks engineered the final products, and Brownline Tools has since become a strong player in the digital tools segment.

MAKE THAT JOINT EXPERIMENTS

One of the more radical ideas of this process is the concept of experimenting in tandem. This process isn't one that most large companies consider, but it can have tremendous impact on the outcome and the partnership.

I was involved in managing a new strategic relationship between a leading consumer health company and a smaller consumer product business, involving several new technologies. Both companies acknowledged that they had tremendous potential for working together in multiple areas, yet they faced difficult choices in terms of where to focus for the best payback. The discussion quickly became opinion driven, dominated by the issues of who should get what.

So we changed the dynamic by leading both parties through a process of collectively studying the external opportunities to better understand the market gaps and the fit with these two companies. With a short list of promising "hunting grounds" in place, we then helped them develop very structured learning experiments in which their key assumptions could be tested and they could determine what was the least amount of work needed to validate the market opportunities and their potential joint solutions.

This market-facing approach and focus on lean experimentation were instrumental in moving this partnership forward to co-development.

CO-VENTURING AND DIFFERING VIEWS OF RISK

What do these strategies look like in action? Stories that show us are all around. For example, in my business, I work with both large companies and entrepreneurs in creating and managing innovation initiatives and ventures. I've dealt with multiple situations with entrepreneurs, where there were differing views, and I believe the following example illustrates an important point for both corporate executives and inventors or technology entrepreneurs. That point is the need to recognize and proactively address the differences in perceived risk as entrepreneurs and large companies begin co-development and commercialization of big ideas.

A technology entrepreneur I know invented a breakthrough wearable device for measuring caloric burn during activities. In this area, the market is ripe for solutions that help consumers understand their energy balance (calories in minus calories out equals weight gain/loss). The technology actually works, even for resistance/weight training, and, more importantly, it can be developed at a low cost and allow for a compelling price point. It passed my key tests for marketable innovation: (1) it addressed a true unmet consumer need; (2) it was an innovative, unique solution; and (3) the marketplace opportunity was there (timing, price point, business model, etc.).

Yet, in spite of this, the entrepreneur's company has languished for years even though he reached the negotiation stage with numerous large branded companies for licensing and/or acquisition. So why no deals? The entrepreneur was insulted by companies trying to steal the idea away with little to nothing upfront. Companies likely view this entrepreneur as naive and without an understanding of business. The entrepreneur views an upfront payment as a reasonable request, given the millions that he has invested in the company to date and the size of the long-term market opportunity.

The reality: each side is valuing the opportunity from a unique assessment of the risk. Large companies have much less tolerance for risk than do entrepreneurs. This may be obvious, but I see too many situations where both sides are neither facing that reality nor looking for creative ways around the disconnect.

This same scenario plays out over and over and over.

WHAT TO DO?

My advice in these situations: get out into the market in a small way. Prove out the opportunity from both a product standpoint and a consumer benefit standpoint. Create a demand and establish viability, and then find large partners to apply brands and broader distribution in order to scale up the business. However, I wouldn't advise this in all situations. Often, licensing the I/P is the absolute right approach and allows all players to do what they do best: inventors invent, and large companies develop and market. But in cases of both high technology and market risk, someone needs to build and develop the market in a smaller way as a first step. This might mean taking it to market directly (as the inventors of the Dr. Johns Spin Brush did prior to approaching P&G) or finding smaller, more entrepreneurial partners initially (instead of focusing on large companies).

My advice to large companies in these situations is to look for creative ways that minimize their risk while not losing the opportunity. Solutions such as limited upfront fees, licensing initially only for a narrow segment, or even licensing out the brand (of course only if this makes sense) are all avenues for minimizing risk while leveraging external sources of innovation.

None of these players' views of risk are wrong. The mistake, as in these cases, is in not recognizing and addressing others' perceptions of risk. Remember that your potential partners' perception of risk is not just a perception but their reality—and thereby yours.

FROM INCUBATION TO INTEGRATION

In my current business, I had a new product/service executive from a major utility approach me with a request for support in convincing his management to scale up what he saw as disruptive strategic initiatives that were critical to the organization's success and ones that he had demonstrated via pilots. He had the support of the CEO, yet the business general managers and other levels of middle management took a more risk-averse view of these opportunities. This executive saw the others as roadblocks and was compelled to bring them over to his way of thinking or go around them if needed.

The problem was that this wasn't with one or two individuals; this risk-averse mindset was a broadly held view across most of the management team. I advised him to stop trying to take on organizational culture change within his program and instead adapt his approach to innovation in a way that matched his organization's tolerance for risk. Pushing incubation and risk to outside partners is one way to accomplish this. Of course, you're relinquishing some upside, but it's a trade-off you can leverage to de-risk and accelerate ventures that would otherwise remain stuck and likely never see the light of day.

Incubating transformative opportunities is hard. Doing it in partnership with others adds another level of complexity.

In this chapter, I've presented three models of corporate/startup incubation that are being adapted in a wide variety of ways by companies. You'll likely want to adapt different approaches in different situations; you don't need to set up your organization to support one approach at the expense of others.

In the next chapter, I'll talk about integrating opportunities that have achieved product/market fit through experimentation and incubation and are ready for scale-up leveraging of the strengths of the corporation.

INTEGRATE: TRANSITION AND SCALE

Just as growth opportunities and ventures seem ready to make a leap forward, things can fall apart.

It's a common occurrence: a corporation and its entrepreneurial partner have gotten through the hard work of incubating a new venture, yet somehow, right at this critical juncture, connections fray, vision falters, and the initiative stalls.

What's going on? This turbulence can come just as an opportunity is moving from incubating to scaling. This is the moment of integration. It's the point at which the partners need to stop focusing exclusively on proving out a business model and move attention to scaling the business and bringing the innovation into the corporation's fold.

Successful innovation is about more than inventing or discovering something new. Smart companies understand the power of marketing at scale to move new products and services to the masses. History is full of examples of companies introducing breakthrough ideas, with larger companies coming in later to steal the market through a focus on ease of use, price, and distribution. Think back to Tappan, the company that introduced the first microwave oven for consumers in 1955. When Sharp and Samsung entered the market, they won on price, and the market expanded rapidly. Another example lies in MP3 players, where a broad set of highly innovative companies, from Rio to Creative, was introducing MP3 players and disrupting the Walkmans and portable CD players that came before. However, the market remained small and fragmented. When Apple entered with a new business model, player, and user experience, it changed the game. Apple dominated the market, and the market exploded.

This chapter deals with how to begin leveraging the brands, distribution, and corporate smarts of the enterprise to take big ideas and scale them. Integrating them at the right time and with the right approach are key success factors in ventures' survival and growth. We'll provide guidelines on how to manage this integration and avoid some common potential pitfalls. But we'll start with a brief discussion of the opportunity that corporates have for early acquisition of promising startups before significant VC funding comes into the picture.

EARLY EXITS

When it's time to transition and scale strategic growth initiatives, you may have already structured a deal with the external partner in the discover or define phases, perhaps a license agreement or license option. If you incubated the opportunity via a collaboration or co-development agreement, then the integration phase will definitely trigger deal time. At this point, you've validated product/market fit and have had experience in market experimentation with the business model and go-to-market strategy.

Deals can take many forms. You may decide to acquire the technology or startup, structure a license agreement for the technology, or simply sign a supply agreement or long-term collaboration agreement with the partner.

If you've had an option agreement in place, this may be the time that you exercise that option and complete the transaction.

I want to make some points related to the corporate exits for startups and a few of the challenges that venture capital funding can sometimes present for venture-funded startups. These issues are relevant to corporate executives because I believe that corporates are an increasingly attractive alternative for entrepreneurial firms and startups that are caught in the chasm between early-stage seed funding and traditional venture capital funding. More and more, startups are recognizing the value of selling directly to these large companies versus pursuing venture capital money and/or IPOs to take the business to another level.

The lean startup movement has spurred a new model and mindset of venture creation that are focusing less on IPOs and more on building fundamentally sound startups on limited budgets. I believe that more and more venture investors (angels and otherwise) will increasingly wake up to the opportunities to connect with corporate partners for successful and faster exits.

In many ways the traditional venture capital model is broken. Figures vary, but most returns come from about 10%–20% of the investments in a typical venture capital portfolio. Partly because of this hit rate and partly because of the large sums of money that VC funds have raised, they are pushed to swing for the fences. The implication? Basil Peters in his book *Early Exits* highlights how VC-funded startups are being dissuaded from early exits as the VCs shoot for 10× or even 30× returns, where many profitable exits could have happened at 5–10×.

A Kauffman Foundation study looked at the change in exits when VCs invested. What did this study find? With VC money (vs. angel or friends and family money) there were:

- 10% more failures

- Nearly 20% fewer 1–5× exits

- 5% more 5–10× exits

- Only 1% more 10–30× exits

According to a recent survey by DLA Piper, "Tech executives believe that corporate investors bring something to the table that VC funds do not: operational expertise. VC's also take themselves out of the game by demanding unreasonable terms."

So, for an increasing number of startups, traditional venture capital can both lower the probability of exit and extend time to exit from three to five years to more like 10 to 12 years. What does this all mean? Corporate venture capital and corporate partnerships are an increasingly important alternative to traditional venture capital. Big companies are now competing for these ready-to-scale startups. If you're a startup, large companies are now even more attractive as an exit strategy.

Even Google, well known for its large acquisitions such as Waze and Motorola Mobility, is focused on smaller transactions. According to Charles Rim, a Google M&A principle at the time, "90% plus of our transactions are small transactions. So that would be less than 20 people, less than $20 million, and that is truly the sweet spot."

INTEGRATION GONE WRONG

While corporate exits are an attractive alternative for startups today, these exits come with their own set of challenges. Most importantly, integrating startups into established companies can result in killing the value that you've acquired if you don't effectively manage the transition or recognize the often very different cultures and mindsets that drive startups in comparison to large established corporate teams.

Yahoo and Flickr

When Yahoo acquired Flickr in 2005, there were great expectations and opportunities for Yahoo to benefit greatly from this successful photo-sharing site and for Flickr to benefit from the resources and scale of Yahoo in ensuring long-term survival and growth.

Instead, Flickr is almost an afterthought today, having lost its luster and its market share: Facebook encroached on its core social sharing market, Instagram stole the on-the-go photo-sharing market, and Dropbox and others became the de facto standard for cloud-based archiving of photos. How did it happen?

From numerous published articles and stories relayed by ex-employees, one of the core reasons for the implosion of Flickr was the poor integration effort and ongoing bureaucracy imposed on Flickr in the years since the initial acquisition. One of these senior-level employees estimated that 85% of the unit's time was spent dealing with the Yahoo bureaucracy and only 15% spent toward innovation for the once-loyal user base that brought them to this point. As Yahoo starved the unit from investment and resources, Facebook stole much of Flickr's core market share.

Another issue arose in how Flickr was measured and incentivized in the years after the purchase by Yahoo. Because the initial deal was struck with the corporate development group at Yahoo, this group essentially managed the Flickr unit and focused almost exclusively on hitting the deal milestones that both sides had initially negotiated. So instead of looking forward to the market and innovation, both corporate development and the Flickr team focused on the engineering and service requirements demanded by the acquisition integration team. Even the cost of the Yahoo oversight was charged back to the unit, further hampering its ability to invest in innovation.

Ultimately, Flickr lost its focus on its core user community, who saw competing solutions doing a better job delivering on their needs. In hindsight, even the objectives for the acquisition were misaligned. Flickr was a social sharing site, and its user base was a loyal community. According to a senior Yahoo executive at the time, Yahoo's priority was not on the community; it was to monetize the image index. So when Yahoo imposed the rule that all Flickr users needed a Yahoo sign-on, it created a nightmare for the community and accelerated the departure of users.

Flickr could have been an important platform for Yahoo in its quest to compete with Facebook and Google. Instead, Yahoo's mismanagement of the integration and culture of Flickr accelerated its decline and the departure of the core of the team behind it.

Black & Decker: The Dangers of Licensing Innovation

In 2006, Black & Decker Corporation (now Stanley Black & Decker) announced its acquisition of Vector Products, based in south Florida, where I live, for $160 million. Vector was founded only 10 years prior and made a name for itself by leveraging its technology strengths in battery charging into a broad line of innovative charging, lighting, and emergency-related consumer products. It established itself as an innovator and gained distribution at major mass retailers including Walmart, Target, Home Depot, and Sam's Club, among others.

One of the key milestones in Vector's growth was its license of the Black & Decker brand for a unique line of emergency-power chargers, inverters, and lights. I don't know firsthand what went on within Black & Decker's walls during the initial decision making on licensing the brand to Vector. Whether it was intentional or not, Black & Decker executed a winning strategy of using brand licensing as a tool for entering a new market and creating a new growth platform.

On the surface, Black & Decker's purchase of Vector was a simple accretive acquisition to fuel growth. But Black & Decker was also possibly looking to expand into these technologies and categories in a bigger way. As a method of both hedging risk and shortening the time line, brand licensing can be a smart way to conduct a strategic experiment of sorts.

As large companies look to strategic innovation to create new sources of growth, licensing one's brand to a technology innovator in the category provides the benefit of speed and brand leverage while minimizing the risk to the parent company. Of course, brand licensing can't be taken lightly, either, and due diligence and license management play an important role. But if your company has the capability and mindset for strategic licensing out of its brands, consider licensing one of the key potential tools in your strategy as well.

Conversely, if you're an entrepreneur seeking to license your technology and products to large established companies, obtaining a brand license from a target acquirer provides a great way for both sides to test the waters, though the brand licensee bears more risk in this model.

A key lesson from this story: when acquiring innovation from the outside, make sure you don't destroy the very thing you're acquiring.

Success in leveraging external innovation isn't just about *finding* technologies, products, and startups for new sources of growth. The hardest part, especially when it's an acquisition of a company (vs. a product or technology), is often in successfully *integrating* the acquired company.

Black & Decker had licensed its brand to Vector for several years, and the licensing-to-acquisition path actually looked like a smart move on B&D's part. It had afforded B&D an opportunity to leverage one of its strengths (brand) into a new but related category (emergency preparedness and inverters/chargers) with limited risk.

Well, just a few years after the acquisition, I started to hear word locally that Vector had begun to lay off a significant number of employees (though it said it planned none when it announced the acquisition) as the business had struggled under Black & Decker. Laid-off employees talked of an entrepreneurial company that struggled to retain that culture under the process-driven, disciplined approaches of Black & Decker. New products suffered, the speed of innovation slowed, and large-company best practices turned out not to be the best thing after all.

INTEGRATION DONE RIGHT
P&G and the Spin Brush

One classic example from the business archives comes from P&G, when the company acquired the Spin Brush from John Osher and his entrepreneurial partners in 2001.

Osher was a serial inventor and had a track record of success with the big companies. Perhaps his biggest was the Spin Pop, a lollipop attached to a battery-powered plastic handle, in which the candy spun at the press of a button. Hasbro had purchased the spinning lolly for millions, and now Osher and his team were on the hunt for another way to monetize the handheld rotary technology.

The idea hit them as Osher and team strolled the aisles of Walmart, a brainstorming process that had served them well in the past. That's where they spotted the long shelf of electric toothbrushes: Sonicare, Interplak, and more. Most were pricey, $50 and up. What if, they wondered, they could make a $5 electric brush using the Spin Pop technology? They spent 18 months designing a brush that wouldn't cost more than $5, batteries included.

In 2000, 10 million Dr. John's Spin Brush units sold. Armed with those results, Osher went to Procter & Gamble.

The sale to P&G was uniquely structured and included an upfront sum with a three-year earn-out period, plus one more twist: Osher and his two partners agreed to join the company for the early stages of scale-up and integration into P&G. Their mission was to keep the SpinBrush venture entrepreneurial.

SpinBrush marked P&G's quickest global rollout ever. Meanwhile, the entrepreneurs walked away with $475 million. (Yes, you read that right.) For a toothbrush! Why such a high multiple? Because Osher and his team were smart enough and confident enough to base their earn out on sales results.

MemberHealth

In 2003, when the federal government decided to create a prescription drug plan for Medicare, a small company called MemberHealth threw its name in the ring, along with the big guys, to administer the program as Part D sponsors. Up to that point, Charles Hallberg and his 13-person startup had been focused on helping seniors get discounts on prescription drugs.

By 2007, MemberHealth earned the number 1 spot on the *Inc.* 500 list, with three-year growth of 20,129%. (Yes, you also read that right.) Hallberg's decision led to MemberHealth's becoming the fourth-largest Medicare Part D sponsor, accounting for 7% of all enrollments. Universal American Financial acquired the company for $630 million that same year.

But MemberHealth's growth and exit can be partly explained by its ability to partner with large companies for scale and by positioning itself uniquely to be an accretive acquisition by another healthcare insurance company. Hallberg knew when he entered the Part D sponsor program that he couldn't do it alone, so early on, MemberHealth formed a partnership with a very large federal contractor, Computer Sciences Corporation (CSC), and the two companies applied for the federal Part D partnership together. MemberHealth won a contract and found its niche by focusing on independent pharmacies, a channel ignored by most of the major players. A few years later, during the next phase of the program, CSC opted out at the last minute but had already given MemberHealth the head start it needed to compete on its own, so it submitted and again won a contract from the federal government, in part due to the success of its partnership with CSC.

Hallberg also began engaging and positioning his business for partnership (or sale) with major insurance providers in whose sides he was already becoming a thorn, including Universal American, a large health and life insurance company. He knew that MemberHealth's unique focus on the independent pharmacy market was a new growth opportunity for large insurance companies. Also, the additional offerings and support that a firm such as Universal American could provide would be valuable to the pharmacy channel.

Hallberg eventually sold MemberHealth to Universal American for $630 million—quite a windfall for the successful entrepreneur. In a great move by Universal American, it was able to convince Hallberg to stay on as CEO of the pharmacy business, which he held until his retirement—a retirement that was short-lived in Sarasota, Florida. His angel investment in a direct-selling company, LiveSmart360, led to his stepping into the CEO role once again.

Hallberg understands the formula. It includes good relationships with vendors, suppliers, and potential partners; a strong foothold in a niche market that is poised for growth; visionary leaders who know their businesses and aren't afraid to take smart risks; and, yes, definitely elements of luck and timing.

Google and Nest

When Google acquired Nest for $3.2 billion in 2014, there was little doubt that Google saw Nest as its spearhead into the smart home and intelligent consumer device markets. At least in the early integration, Google seemed to be supporting Nest as a standalone business that had access to the vast resources of Google but could still retain its own identity, culture, and strategies to compete in a fast-evolving smart home competitive marketplace.

Tony Fadell and his Nest team meet on a bimonthly basis with Larry Page and engage with different areas of Google to explore how these new capabilities might improve or redirect Nest's existing development road map. But Nest is thus far still run as an independent business within Google. Case in point: even with Google's clear emphasis on consumer data collection, Nest has maintained that no commingling of user data with Google is happening and that Nest's management team is making its own decisions on strategic direction. Over time, I would definitely predict that Google will reap the synergies of its acquisition, but for now, both for avoiding consumer backlash and for ensuring Google doesn't destroy Nest's inherent value, it is emphasizing autonomy over integration and doing so successfully.

WHAT CAN WE LEARN?

Given this group of examples, let's talk about some steps companies can take to ensure that they don't kill the very things they're acquiring: innovations and the innovative cultures that create them.

I discussed the importance of successful integration of innovation acquisitions. It's a timely topic because, increasingly, open innovation is being expanded from simply acquiring/licensing technologies to more situations of acquiring small companies as a platform for innovation-driven growth.

So what makes for a successful integration?

First, it requires recognition upfront of the cultural differences and sensitivity (especially on the large company's part) to those differences.

Next, it needs an integration strategy that deals with not just the first 90 days (this is the part most companies do well) but also the first 900 days (meaning that companies need to recognize that integration is a three-year process, not a three-month process).

All players must show a willingness to allow exceptions to the rules; successful integrations allow these smaller entrepreneurial entities to sometimes play by different rules concerning financial reporting, bonus/incentive structure, and even reporting relationships. Senior leadership must show an ability to accept and support ambiguity and dual systems, at least for a period of time.

Most of all, a critical factor is the selection of a strong leader (who has credibility with and strong support of the parent company CEO) for the acquired business who understands and can relate to both the parent company's culture, systems, and approaches and the acquired company's unique entrepreneurial style. Often this will turn out not to be the original founder/CEO but rather someone who has had experience in both entrepreneurial and large corporate environments (likely the parent company).

ANOTHER SOLUTION: BUILD NEW BRANDS

Should these new growth platforms be extensions of existing brands or new brands? It's often too easy for brands to think of new growth platforms as extensions of their major brands. They should also be thinking of these disruptive new businesses as opportunities to create a new brand.

Authors Al and Laura Ries in "The Origin of Brands" use the theories of Darwinian selection as an analogy to how companies should create and grow brands. Rather than use line extensions to support existing brands (accepted practice), they assert that companies need to branch out (diverge) in search of unique opportunities for growth.

They argue that companies must foster innovation and novelty rather than simply leverage name recognition. It's temping, of course, to rely on previous wins. It feels safe, smart. But the authors advise a company to introduce a new brand and create a distinctive identity for it, much as

Hanes did with its L'eggs pantyhose. Hanes targeted supermarkets because department stores were declining; interestingly, instead of extending its old brand, the company unveiled a clever new package, a new name, and a brand-new brand. Strong sales followed.

This bold new brand effort allowed Hanes to dominate its category. A safer brand extension route might not have produced the necessary momentum. Many big companies—Motorola, Dell—followed the safe route of line extension right into the doldrums.

FINDING A HOME FOR BREAKTHROUGHS: KEY STEPS

As we've seen, incubating a big idea or proving out a new business model is only half the battle. Successfully scaling the idea and ultimately finding a home for it in the enterprise are what ensure ultimate success. This is where the critical core skills of the corporation from brand building to distribution at scale come into their own. The challenge is in managing this transition in a way that doesn't kill the very thing that you've spent so much time nurturing.

Step 1: Know when to scale and integrate an early-stage opportunity

The inflection point for market-creating products, while very difficult to predict, is where large companies with the right brands and market presence can leverage the work of others to scale a new market at lower risk and lower cost than if they had tried to do it on their own. The benefit of the collective disruption model is that a smart company can engage with startups to experiment at lower risk and cost and then scale the opportunity when a dominant design is becoming established to reap the financial benefit of the market explosion.

So how do you know when the time is right? New markets require the entrepreneurial zeal of startups and their ability to explore and experiment on both the market and technology sides. As more entrants come into a new market, customer uptake is often still small, limited to early adopters and niche markets. Then a dominant design takes hold, often driven by brand, distribution, and price. I would argue that the co-creation model I'm advocating puts you, as the large company, in a great position to see firsthand how the market is evolving and provides a much better viewpoint to know when your brands, price efficiencies, and distribution models are likely to enable rapid scale-up.

Entrepreneurs are natural risk takers, we know. When the initial consumer proposition has been developed and validated and the core business model proven, think about scaling up. Of course, this will vary by industry and segment. For the company to get behind an idea and apply its brands and distribution, along with significant investment to scale an opportunity, much of the market and technology risk must be first addressed in the incubation period. When funding and resources for growth become the core focus, begin the transition to its new parent.

IBM developed and publicized its own criteria for transitioning EBO (emerging business opportunity) ventures into its business lines:

- Strong leadership team in place

- Clear and validated strategy for profit contribution

- Proven customer value proposition

- Early market success

Step 2: Define the right roles during integration, leveraging the strengths of the corporation and the startup

When expanding market presence, the prowess and scale of the large company can absolutely be leveraged to accelerate the growth of a new opportunity. Yet, too many examples exist of large companies exerting too much influence too soon, and the integration and scale-up flounder. A healthcare executive recently related his story to me of the integration of an in-licensed breakthrough technology. While the startup was very capable of managing clinical study design, the large pharmaceutical company wanted to protect its investment (a license deal was in place with milestones for development and launch). The two companies were co-developing this new platform area, but, unfortunately, the pharma company inserted so much governance and reporting requirements for the startup that it became distracted from its core activities. The solution failed in its clinical trials due to a very avoidable design flaw, and the deal evaporated.

Defining roles in ways that leverage the strengths of each of the partners is critical during integration. Often, it makes sense to imbed a startup executive with the team during this period and/or assign a corporate executive to co-locate with the startup during later-stage incubation. I've shared examples of each approach in this book.

Governance should take place at both the executive level, where only milestone-based reporting and engagement should be pursued, and the working level, where peer engagement for the working team can ensure integration at the tactical level. This is too often where it falls apart.

It becomes fairly clear when the startup's management approach no longer is enough to support broader and more sophisticated marketing and growth efforts. The startup team moves from a position of leadership to one of consulting and support during the later period of a transition. Times vary but could be as short as 90 days or as long as a year (in pharma especially).

Step 3: Find the right home, whether setting up a new business unit or integrating into an existing one

By definition, new business creation is whitespace for the large company, even if not new to the world. Whether to integrate the business into an existing business unit or manage it as a unique SBU often comes down to the degree to which core competencies of the parent corporation must be brought to bear to support the business. During my corporate career, I ran a small "orphaned" business unit that depended greatly on shared resources in sales, quality, and distribution. I can tell you that it was a constant battle to gain attention from shared services and to retain some independence, as our channels and go-to-market approach remained unique to us. Eventually, the new business was consolidated into the larger core business, with a dedicated midlevel management team. When this finally came to fruition, nearly all of these problems disappeared.

The other criteria to keep in mind are the growth trajectory and the potential of the business venture. If we're talking about a billion-dollar growth platform, the inefficiency is worth treating the business as a separate unit to enable some degree of autonomy from the parent.

INTEGRATION IS A DANCE

We've seen in this chapter that the integration point is a delicate time in the collaborative disruption process. The key to success is remembering what big companies can—and can't—bring to the table. Too often, innovators view big companies as little more than funding sources. But good integration needs more than money; it needs a collaboration of skills. Big companies bring lots of skills, certainly in the early idea stage, but much more so at this one, when the great idea is ready to scale up and be big.

I've known Stan Lech for a decade, and I've long admired him as a true change agent in a very large company. He has a track record of operating outside of the norms to push an organization forward and pursue big ideas beyond the organization's comfort zone. But he also has a track record of results, and now that he's joined the ranks of the entrepreneurs, he's pursuing big ideas with zeal. Lech is in a unique position to speak to the need for integration between corporates and startups.

STAN LECH,
PRESIDENT, PHARMAMAX (EX-VP GLOBAL WELLNESS R&D FOR GSK)

Stan Lech spent most of his career in large companies and left the comfort of that world to become an entrepreneur. He thinks other corporate executives could learn something by running startups.

Large organizations can often provide too much comfort for executives, and, over time, their sense of urgency and sharpness can diminish.

Once executives lose that "fire in their belly" and revert to "playing it safe to keep their job," it's over. Corporate cultures and a difficult economy can prevent people from taking chances. People feel that they have to be collegial, have to be overly collaborative, have to be agreeable. They don't want to be on the wrong side.

I think a way out of this is for large companies to partner with small companies and entrepreneurs who are quite radical in their innovation and radical in their thought. They can help push the large organization into new spaces or look at problems and opportunities differently.

Engage people who are strategic thinkers, who know how to make things happen, and who have ideas that are better than a 50/50 chance. There are a lot of ideas and people that fit this profile—you just need to know where to look. Large companies should be seeking out these situations and putting their money and their scale behind them.

Large companies should absolutely be investing in incubators and proven entrepreneurs. There is real opportunity, and entrepreneurs with a proven track record and knowledge in the large company's space can be very valuable. These folks know how to effectively communicate, collaborate, constructively challenge, and navigate the corporate environment.

Small companies often have great ideas, emerging technologies, and speed but lack the resources to scale. Large companies have resources and scale but need ideas and more agility. In reality, it can be simple to solve. Large companies need to have the right people in the decision-making process and have clear internal processes in place to leverage the opportunities with small- to medium-sized companies.

With so much opportunity riding on the success of both large and small companies, the first ones that can put together a model of collaboration that works are going to outpace their competitors for sure.

My current venture, PharmaMax, is a small China-based pharmaceutical company focused on partnering with large multinationals from the beginning. We have a unique model for accessing the China market and the capabilities to be a partner to large companies in accelerating development and commercialization. We're definitely trying to build the type of collective disruption model that you're talking about. We can develop the products and get them into the complex China market and then integrate the business with the multinational, and we become a strategic supply source.

In the past two years running smaller ventures, I have become even more urgent and deliberate in my interactions and have become relentless in driving harder for business results. I think almost every executive running a large company should be sent off to start his or her own business or new venture for two to three years. When he or she comes back to the organization, these new skills and practices can be embedded back into the culture. To do this will require a big change in talent development practices within large companies. Being outside the corporate bubble makes you tougher, it clarifies your vision and mission in life, and it certainly sharpens your human and professional instincts needed to survive and then thrive. Success in this situation (running a new venture) is the real acid test in my mind.

Large companies need leaders who will run the business with the passion and urgency of entrepreneurs. We need a fusion between the skills and capability of both large and small companies. This will definitely require creativity and new types of collaboration models.

Stan Lech is currently president of PharmaMax Corporation, a growth-stage pharmaceutical company in New Jersey and Taizhou, China; he's also an advisor to numerous other healthcare ventures. Previously, he was VP of global wellness R&D for GlaxoSmithKline Consumer Healthcare and before that GSK's VP of innovation.

We can have access to the best ideas and startups in the world, but if our creative corporate executives leave and we don't have visionary leadership inside our corporate walls, all of these great external opportunities that come inside will be squandered. Success requires a delicate balance of skills inside and outside the enterprise. In our next and final chapter, we'll talk more about the leadership challenge of making this approach move smoothly and where it's all heading.

10

LEADERSHIP IN THIS NEW ERA

In this final chapter, we explore how collaboration, and, specifically, collective disruption, is changing the way we work in profound ways. We'll discuss the future of working and the imminent death of today's organizational models—to be replaced by organizational structures and new skill sets that embrace more fluid cross-organization collaboration. In short, we'll talk about what a company needs to do on the inside before it can successfully engage in collective disruption on the outside. Some of the adjustments are physical, such as structural org chart issues, but many, many more are about changes in mindset. Leadership in this new era begins with the mind.

LOSING CONTROL

Corporate management has traditionally focused on control. In a world of collaboration, control is impossible. What we are really striving for is order. In this new era, companies need to think differently. We're now dealing with a vastly more complex management model that cuts across organizations and requires you to put some amount of faith in people over whom you have little to no control. Scary.

"Not invented here" (NIH) is a term often used in discussing resistance within the organization to more open models of innovation. NIH is real; I've been there myself. If you think about this from the perspective of interdependence, maybe this NIH we sometimes see is less about pride of ownership and more about fear of losing control and fear of trusting external partners. Maybe it's a sign of an organization that's at the stage of independence but hasn't yet achieved the stage of interdependence.

When I was the VP of new products at Sunbeam, I was under a lot of pressure to deliver a lot of breakthrough products, quickly and with limited budgets. I had an organization of a hundred people in new product marketing, engineering, industrial design, and quality, as well as our Hong Kong development team. Yet it just wasn't enough. We used some externally generated ideas but still developed internally. I remember one of my directors coming to me in desperation: "Mike, we can't keep this up and get to the kind of numbers that you're asking for. We have to leverage these inventors and our suppliers to do more of this."

I remember talking to my wife about it and my fears of letting go of some of this control. It felt very unnatural to lose control of large portions of this to outside partners while I was still accountable. My wife said to me, "Mike, remember how you always tell your team leaders to stop being musicians and become conductors? Isn't this the same thing?"

So over the next year, we ended up rethinking our roles and then remaking our organization. We became conductors. We continued to do key internal R&D, but we put a lot more effort into finding inventions and outside development partners.

I mentioned in the introduction that we went from launching 10 new products in that first year to more than 150 by the end of the second. Well, we did it with fewer people and a smaller budget, by letting go of some control and gaining support from a broader network.

I used this same approach when I became SVP/GM of Sunbeam's health businesses. It helped us take a $100-million division that had lost money for the previous four straight years and make it profitable within 18 months.

Losing some control over the process is scary. We were forced into it, but it is central to any company learning how to leverage the entrepreneurial ecosystem to fuel growth.

ORDER VERSUS CONTROL

When I talk about giving up control, I'm obviously not suggesting anarchy. Smart leaders in this new interconnected and complex business environment have learned to put their trust not in control but in order.

Nature abounds with examples of what's often called "swarm intelligence." Think of migrating birds or even termites. These entities lack a centralized point of control, yet they are able to move forward as a group. Why? They may lack orders for every move they make, but they operate within a few core rules.

Imagine this now in a human context. Jazz improvisation and comedy improv are both great examples of multiple agents acting in coordinated approaches without central leadership. In both cases, basic rules exist for operating together that maximize the opportunity for success and mitigate risks of mistakes that are bound to happen.

We have seen this in a business context as well. The evolution of the TED Talks illustrates ceding control in a real way. When Richard Saul Wurman originally started the TED Conferences (focused on Technology, Entertainment, and Design) back in 1984, they were very much a curated and exclusive invitation-only group. When Chris Anderson acquired the rights to TED in 2001, it became a nonprofit, and he clearly ceded some of his control to a large community of supporters. Posting TED talks online was considered highly risky to the brand and its exclusivity.

Yet within a few years, TED's focus on "ideas worth spreading" clearly was being embraced by the world and served only to strengthen the brand. By 2012, TED talks had been viewed on the Internet more than one billion times.

As TEDx events now expand, Anderson is taking a different kind of risk in allowing local organizers to run events under the TED branding. He's entrusting the collective intelligence of this community, and it's generally working. Exceptions exist, such as the now publicly debunked TEDx talk "Vortex-Based Mathematics" by Randy Powell; however, while this particular incident and others have caused problems for TED, they are the risks one takes when losing some amount of control. For TED, it remains an experiment that, on balance, seems to be working.

Netflix is probably one of the best examples of a company that's embracing collective intelligence and distributed control of the enterprise. For example, Netflix's vacation policy states simply that there is no vacation policy or tracking. Company executives have said that the policy reflects a company credo: responsible people thrive on freedom. Hires are made with an eye toward the ability to succeed in this free environment. With the right people, instead of a process-driven culture, one can create a culture of creativity and self-discipline, freedom and responsibility.

THE VIRTUAL ENTERPRISE

The future of growth and innovation is not via a singular focus on internally developed ideas nor is it big companies simply acquiring external technologies and commercializing them. The coming virtual enterprise is one that's connected in a web of relationships with customers, suppliers, and a curated group of entrepreneurs and startups who matter to each other—all of this supported by crowdsourcing and open innovation for access to even larger groups of ideas and resources in the world at large.

I've long thought of the film industry as a great analogy for the business environment of the future. My brother-in-law, Jim Bigham, happens to be an award-winning filmmaker, so I've been able to witness some of this in action over the years as he's established and leveraged a long series of relationships in developing commercials, documentaries, and feature films. Whenever a project is being developed, he pulls together the resources to tackle it or, similarly, is pulled into others' projects.

I worked with Jim and some of his network on a commercial video shoot for the Fit & Fresh line of consumer products I mentioned earlier. Even as we were discussing the commercial project, Jim was recruiting a world-class videographer, food stylists, researchers, and other creatives who were able to quickly come together and execute the project seamlessly, on a tight budget, and with existing relationships that allowed them to function as a well-oiled machine (or an old married couple, depending on the day).

Jim is also a member of a select, invitation-only community of about 100 of the top film and production leaders from 45 countries around the globe, called IQ (the International Quorum of Motion Picture Producers). They epitomize the concept of a curated community of collaborators. Each year, the producer/members come together to share ideas and build relationships. Throughout the year, they are a powerful network for finding, vetting, and collaborating with resources around the world for filmmaking and television work. The organization invites the individual, not the company, and this membership follows that individual even through job changes (though nearly all are owners or CEOs).

Imagine the power of similar groups of experts in new business creation coming together to identify, incubate, and commercialize breakthrough opportunities and businesses in ways that blur the lines between large corporations and startup ecosystems.

Cisco is a company that is moving quickly toward the vision of the virtual enterprise and is embracing collaboration and co-creation at every level. Kate O'Keeffe leads a new Cisco initiative to co-create in real time with customers, partners, and startups in strategic focus areas such as the "Internet of Everything."

KATE O'KEEFFE,
LEAD, CISCO HYPER-INNOVATION LIVING LABS

Kate O'Keeffe is leading a group that is engaging with Cisco's partners and customers of all sizes to co-create transformative innovations that no single company could successfully tackle alone.

My department is called Cisco Hyper-Innovation Living Labs. Complementary to our existing R&D facilities and incubators, our Living Labs emphasize live customer involvement, live testing, and lean startup principles. We're creating new partnership models with other companies to tackle difficult and shared problems, especially those problems that need community or networked solutions to be effective and seamless, like the Internet of Everything (IoE).

It can be tempting for those of us in innovation leadership to jump into an open innovation model without considering the capability gap involved in that shift. Innovating directly with customers and partners requires fundamentally different muscles. I don't mean innovating with customers in terms of doing a focus group or asking someone's opinion. I'm talking about real customer innovation where that customer is taking some form of shared risk with the enterprise.

It's very easy for us to say, "We're going to incorporate startups in our work. We're going to collaborate with our customers." It's easy to set these directions without thinking deeply about your organization's capability and preparedness to do so.

Knowing which parts of your company have built these sorts of muscles can be a powerful way to manage innovation risk. You don't want to threaten your innovation efforts by engaging with the parts of your business that are not ready for that way of working.

I've been working in partnership with our president, Rob Lloyd, whose remit includes leading deep transformational organization-wide engagement around key innovation challenges. The Internet of Everything is Cisco's key big bet at the moment. We believe that the market opportunity globally for economies across the world is *approximately $19 trillion and that the value of this shift toward the Internet of Everything is going to be as big as the Internet has been to this point.*

Machine-to-machine communication, people-to-machine communication, and data-driven decision making are concepts that can really have a dramatic impact. However, the Internet of Everything is not a concept that is easily accessible to everybody in the company.

We designed an approach to drive significant and rapid innovation in the organization and aligned it to that topic of the Internet of Everything. It has helped us increase understanding, comprehension, and adoption of those ideas and strategies across the corporation.

In front of 70,000–80,000 staff across Cisco, Rob launched an innovation challenge that invited deep collaboration across the corporation. The challenge took place over seven days, and we had massive participation, almost 15,000 participants over that period. Over 500 ideas were collected in seven days. Downloads of Cisco's "Internet of Everything" playbook went from about 80 downloads prior to this innovation challenge to several thousand downloads at the end of the competition period. This was a real pivot point. That's enterprise collaboration. We're also collaborating externally.

Cisco's entire go-to-market method is through channel partners. For the $70–$80 billion that we turn over every year, it's almost entirely in the hands of external partners and external technology and telecommunication providers who offer Cisco equipment to their customers. In our case, we have this rich history of partnering with others to deliver value to customers, and as a result we have really strong muscles for leveraging and brokering the sorts of deals that are needed to drive a networked innovation model.

A core part of my role is bringing together groups of non-competing companies to undertake year-long innovation engagements aligned to particular topic areas. It is a facilitated innovation partnership not just with Cisco but also with each other.

It's a four-quarter customer cohort approach whereby quarter one is devoted to discovery with facilitated sessions, along with primary market data and research for the group. Cisco has incredible resources when it comes to thought leadership and primary data that we can share with customers. But also as part of that discovery, we explore the member organizations themselves and look to surface assets that are hidden within those organizations that can be surfaced and shared across the group. Under strict confidentiality we help facilitate the exposure of those unconnected assets where new value could be created.

In the second quarter, we focus on option generation. That's when we generate ideas and leverage a range of tools to supply a diverse series of options from workshops to companywide innovation challenges to hackathon activities. Unique to this process are searches for relevant startups that match our particular challenge criteria. We work to leverage Cisco's Silicon Valley footprint and our deep relationships with the startup community here in order to identify companies that align with some of the opportunities that we've identified as part of the discovery phase. Cisco has $2.2 billion externally invested through our own venture capital vehicle and a deep history of acquisitions, with almost 180 companies brought into Cisco over the last 30 years. Not only do the startups themselves provide incredible opportunities for idea generation, but Cisco has access to incredible data about what's happening in the technology marketplace about where dollars are moving. It can be a great predictor of future shifts.

The final two quarters of our customer cohort approach will be focused on incubation. Can we take the ideas we've been working on and design an appropriate mechanism to incubate them? Can we structure the collaboration agreements and joint ventures that are needed in order to support those options that have been explored so far? Can we identify startups that are aligned to these explorations and are interested in partnering with companies like ours to drive a rapid outcome to market?

These are CEO-to-CEO relationships across four to eight very sizable corporations, so a very big undertaking. We're humbled by the ambition of what we're taking on here. But Cisco has a strong pedigree of co-creating with customers in this way. We believe that this kind of innovation is the best way for us to deliver the results that we need in the areas that lend themselves to a networked innovation approach such as IOE.

Kate O'Keeffe is the lead for Cisco's Hyper-Innovation Living Labs. She was also the global leader of the Services Innovation Excellence Center at Cisco, where her innovation programs were recognized with an M-Prize by *Harvard Business Review* and McKinsey & Company.

IT TAKES A COLLECTIVE

New models of the virtual enterprise are emerging that can show us the future of collaboration. Headed by a passionate leader in Amro Albanna, ieCrowd is launching a series of disruptive new businesses in a variety of health and life science areas, all based on a networked model of commercializing university discoveries. Its first venture, Kite, is bringing to market a breakthrough discovery that can disrupt the mosquito's ability to detect carbon dioxide—making humans virtually invisible to the insects. Imagine the implications for mosquito-borne diseases that claim millions of lives around the world.

ieCrowd is building an impressive network, not only with universities but also with industry partners, funding sources and expertise to support the mission of impacting lives around the world. For Kite, it leveraged the crowd of Indiegogo to raise $557,000 (against a goal of $75,000) with more than 11,000 backers.

Kite and ieCrowd are great examples of collective intelligence combined with a purpose-driven mission. Both are inspiring to me. Collective disruption isn't all about a single company leveraging the startup ecosystem; it's about the power of collaborative groups of all types coming together to achieve amazing things.

In another enlightening example of this collective approach, Medtronic has partnered with two separate startups to bring innovative hearing diagnosis and treatment programs to rural India, with plans to scale in the developing world. Hearing loss is actually one of the most commonly diagnosed health problems in the developing world. Many of these cases could be avoided with early detection and intervention. The Shruti program includes a smartphone-based otoscope from Icarus Design, a telemedicine platform from ClickMedix (an MIT spinout), and a hearing screening protocol developed by Medtronic. The screening takes only three minutes, and images can be sent to ENT specialists in the United States and elsewhere who are overseeing the program. It's a great example of quickly bringing together talent and innovation that's benefitting 70,000 people in India immediately, with the opportunities to scale to millions.

EMERGING ENABLERS FOR COLLECTIVE DISRUPTION

Similar to the beginning of the open innovation movement when marketplaces and intermediaries came on to the scene, I'm seeing a trend under way today of new enabling companies emerging to support collective disruption and new business creation. Many of these models are experiments, but they are strong indicators that this trend is real and growing rapidly. While these new business builders are using a variety of models, the common thread is a focus on value creation that crosses traditional organizational boundaries.

Business Creation Firms: Idealab has been around since 1996 (remember pets.com?), and over that time it has created and operated more than 125 companies with 40 IPOs and acquisitions. A new breed of firms is joining Idealab in the model of leveraging a common infrastructure and developing a core competence in business building. The company above, ieCrowd, is another great example. PureTech in Boston, focused on breakthrough science, is creating a new model for creating a pipeline of life science startups and leveraging relationships (and eventual exits) with big pharma. Nanobiz, Venture2, and Southern Growth Studios in the United States; Bax & Willems in Spain; and other consultancies are creating venturing arms to commercialize ideas that their large corporate clients aren't moving on fast enough.

Hybrid Accelerators: I've discussed the trend of corporations engaging with startup accelerators. New hybrid accelerators are emerging that are designed to curate and pilot startups for corporate partners. Look at Iterate Studios, which focuses on matching e-commerce startups with a consortium of corporations looking to compete against Amazon's $8-billion R&D budget, or Brand Accelerator, a digital incubation program for brands, led by Ed Kaczmarek, who oversaw similar initiatives from inside Mondalēz International. Bionic is a shared accelerator model, based in New York, for corporate venturing using lean startup methods, with premier companies including GE and a group of noncompetitive brands. Accelerators such as the Bakery and Collider, both in London, are built on the model of corporate/startup collaboration.

Entrepreneurs for Hire: My firm, Venture2, has partnered with startup founder groups to source entrepreneurs to help corporates plan and launch their internal ventures. CoFoundersLab (now Onevest) is an example of an entrepreneur network that is looking to corporate partners as a new avenue for placement of its founders. PCDworks in east Texas is a science- and engineering-based invention firm that hires itself out to solve unsolvable problems. Companies bring their teams to PCDworks' remote mountaintop campus to think, invent, and build alongside an amazing team of technologists and makers. OneLeap, based in the United Kingdom, is a firm focused on leveraging its network of entrepreneurs to help leading companies become more entrepreneurial.

Outsourced Venture Development: While it's still a difficult sell to convince corporate leaders to cede control of risky new ventures to the outside, it's happening. My firm is doing this with some of our smaller clients in shared risk/reward compensation models. Prehype in New York and

London partners with large brands and acts as a virtual venture creation team. Allied Minds partners with universities to commercialize leading-edge research into viable new businesses. New Venture Partners, founded by the venture team from Bell Labs, focuses on spinouts from leading companies. All are models focused on value creation.

New Consortium Models: I'm not talking here about industry consortia focused on standards setting. The new breed of consortia is much more pragmatic and commercially focused. Enlight Bio in Boston has built a consortium of pharma companies willing to co-fund and support Enlight Bio's development of transformative life sciences startups at the precompetitive stage. Colabs.com (which I'm involved in) is in the early stages of a new type of cross-company model that is both engaging with startups and encouraging large company partnerships in pursuing breakthrough opportunities.

While these examples might be competitors to my own firm, I'm happy to highlight their existence. The fact that we're not alone in these efforts speaks to the emerging and growing model of collective disruption enablers coming into being. Interestingly, we are finding many of these new players interested in banding together in networks of resources to support each other and provide more scale and acceleration of these pioneering approaches. It's refreshing to see some actual collaboration in the collaborative consulting space.

In my consulting work, I've been involved for some time in helping large companies engage with the startup ecosystem through collaborative summits, demo days, and innovation tours to Silicon Valley, New York, London, and Shanghai to name a few. Most organizations already manage a network of relationships, whether with their supplier base or a close group of long-term strategic partners. But as relationship-based networks gain understanding and importance, the ability to more quickly develop and access expanded relationships with the best innovators in a market space will become a key source of competitive advantage for established companies.

COOPERATION AND COMPETITION

In chapter 3, I talked about the story of the ants and the elephants and their delicate balance of interdependence.

Ecosystems are made up of interdependent groups; they have elements of cooperation and competition. In business ecosystems, especially with collaboration around disruptive opportunities, companies, sometimes even competitors, depend on each other for growth.

As new models such as Enlight Bio demonstrate, even fierce competitors can band together at a precompetitive stage to more efficiently develop transformative platform technologies that can help them all. The competition then comes from who does the best job at commercializing and marketing their solutions. Tesla is doing this by opening up its intellectual property in batteries for others to use.

The winners in the next decade will understand the need to engage with innovation ecosystems and get plugged into the flow of big ideas that come through them. Being integrated in this way helps the corporation better separate the winners from the losers and avoid being overwhelmed or, worse yet, left behind.

BE A GOOD PARTNER

To get big ideas to market, you have to become a good partner for collaboration. Being a good collaboration partner may sound simple or obvious, but in my experience it is one of the most important keys to success in collaborative business creation. It's also where many large companies fail.

Why is it important? Because, as I've said, you're trying to create and manage a highly complex network, and in spite of your best efforts to find partners and ideas . . . it's not enough. You've got to be the kind of partner that attracts the best ideas not because you have the scale and market power to do something with these opportunities but because you've built a reputation as someone who actually does something with it—and not at the expense of your partners.

Large companies that have a reputation as good collaboration partners understand that treating partners with mutual respect (such as being timely and open in due diligence and decision making) and managing initiatives in ways that leverage everyone's strengths are the only ways to go in the long run.

Being a good partner for collaboration will pay dividends for you both in attracting the best ideas and in actually getting something into the market.

COMING FULL CIRCLE

A new and reimagined Kodak emerged from a 20-month Chapter 11 reorganization in September of 2013. Its new focus? Providing disruptive technologies and breakthrough solutions for the packaging and printing commercial markets and other advanced imaging solutions for business. In spite of being a shadow of its former self, the company still has deep expertise and a portfolio of more than 7,500 commercial imaging patents and patent applications.

I wish Kodak success in this new mission. I know from having helped manage Sunbeam Products through bankruptcy that coming out on the other side can be an energizing and motivating position. With fresh capital and the ability to shed massive debt and noncore assets, Kodak can be much more agile and less tied to its legacy while still leveraging the best of its history and skills. I hope that it will embrace a networked approach to it new business model and not try to go it alone.

I also find it exciting and rewarding to see where Jarden Consumer Solutions (previously Sunbeam) is going. The five years I spent helping to manage the prior company successfully through a very difficult period were some of the best (and worst) years of my professional career. Today, I'm watching the next generation of leaders at Jarden take the business to another level by retaining a sense of urgency and avoiding complacency.

Efforts such as its Transformational Innovation group show that the company understands that the next disruption is just around the corner. Now it is committed to being the market disruptor, in part by leveraging the entrepreneurial ecosystem to create new business models and future sources of growth.

MAKING A DIFFERENCE

Throughout this book, I have strived to provide you with a balance of frameworks and tools as well as real-world examples of collective disruption in action. Earlier and deeper collaboration between established corporations and innovation-driven startups and entrepreneurs can accelerate growth and bring to market breakthrough ideas that can change the world. Examples of successful co-creation are already plentiful. Yet there's a huge opportunity remaining for companies and startups to more deliberately and repeatedly work this way. I'm inspired by examples such as the following:

- The original iPod, an iconic transformational innovation, was brought to Apple by Tony Fadell and co-created with a close group of ecosystem partners.

- Tesla came from scrappy startup where it partnered in developing lithium ion battery packs for Daimler and Toyota, then opened its I/P portfolio, and now is building a massive $5-billion gigafactory, which, if successful, could completely change the automotive industry.

- As the next step in Nest's and Google's vision to be the smart home hub, Nest opened its sensors to other apps and devices through its developer program to develop new value-add solutions around the data, with partners ranging from Jawbone to Mercedes-Benz.

- IBM's Emerging Business Opportunities (EBO) has been successful in creating dozens of new businesses and billions in new revenue sources for IBM and is demonstrating a sustainable model for business creation, in large part by leveraging cross-business collaboration across IBM and partners.

- Upstarts such as ieCrowd are taking world-changing technologies out of university labs and creating virtual business teams to bring them to market—innovations, such as the Kite Patch, that can save lives.

These are just a few examples of the many collaborations that are changing the world and changing the way the world innovates.

Ultimately, the message I want to leave you with is that this process begins at home. I hope you come to the same realization as the transformative innovation champions I've introduced you to in these pages. You are capable of tremendous things and can have an amazing impact on your company, your customers, and your career.

We all want to be successful in our careers, but nearly all of us involved in corporate innovation and entrepreneurial endeavors are driven more by a sense of purpose. We want to create something new and meaningful, something that can even improve people's lives. In spite of all of the challenges and naysayers, we want to be champions for big ideas that can change the world.

I believe that there's no shortage of big ideas in this world. My goal with this book hasn't been to help you invent the next big thing; it's to help you realize your vision—to break on through with big ideas and move them forward to reality.

Learn to lose some control and embrace new approaches to collaboration and business building and you'll be amazed by what can happen.

NOTES

A complete list of sources, references, links, and permissions can be found by visiting www.collectivedisruption.com.

This online resource also provides enhanced content, free tools, and additional recommended resources to help you apply collective disruption principles in your own business. Here you can access a complimentary individual or team assessment of key success factors for co-creating transformative innovation. Identify the gaps between where you are and where you want to be; develop strategies to get you there faster and more sustainably.

ACKNOWLEDGMENTS

This book has been a dream of mine for years, and I have a strong network of professional colleagues and friends to thank for help in bringing it to life.

Thank you to the visionary professionals who provided valuable insights and personal stories, allowing me to share them in this book: Dondeena Bradley, Carie Davis, Ricardo dos Santos, Susan Harman, Timothy Howe, Sonny Jandial, Bryan Janeczko, Udaiyan Jatar, Ed Kaczmarek, Dave Knox, Stan Lech, Kyle Nel, Kate O'Keeffe, David Ritter, and Asoka Veeravagu. Brian Gyoerkoe (Venture2) and others also provided important insights that informed this work, even if their words were not included directly.

I could not have written this book without the support and guidance of my editorial expert, Ellen Neuborne. And thank you to the committed team at Jenkins Group, including Jerrold Jenkins, James Kalajian, Leah Nicholson, Yvonne Roehler, Devon Ritter, and Brooke Camfield. Thank you to Paul Grech for the great front cover design and interior illustrations.

Each iteration of the manuscript improved through the reviews and valuable feedback I received from Sarah Miller Caldicott, Eugene Ivanov, Rita Shor, Michael Fruhling, and Marty Daffner, as well as others who provided informal feedback.

To the late Jeff Jacober, my first Venture2 client who became a mentor and friend, thank you for inspiring me to pay it forward in my own life.

Finally, my family puts up with a lot from me, and I definitely tested their patience with this project. To my wife, Theresa, and my children, Jeffrey, Kaitlyn, and Elizabeth, you inspire me every day to be the best person I can be and to be deserving of such a wonderful, loving family.

ABOUT THE AUTHOR

Michael Docherty brings unique perspective to this book, having been an entrepreneur, senior corporate executive, and venture capitalist. He's passionate about the intersection of corporate innovation and entrepreneurship.

As CEO of Venture2, a consulting and new ventures firm, he works with leading brand companies and startups to build innovation ecosystems and commercialize breakthrough new products and businesses. Corporate clients include Unilever, Merck, Pfizer, Cisco, Jarden, and other leading companies.

He has managed venture-backed startups, including a mobile technology innovation network, and was also president of Spencer Trask, a venture investment firm that backed leading collaborative innovation platforms including InnoCentive, inno360, and others. Earlier in his career, Docherty was VP of new products for Sunbeam Appliances (now Jarden) and then VP/GM of Sunbeam Health, during the successful turnaround of the company. Prior to that, he held marketing and technology leadership positions with Ford Motor Company and General Electric.

Docherty holds an MBA degree from Northwestern University's Kellogg School of Management and a BSME degree from Drexel University. He is a highly rated speaker on innovation and corporate venturing and an active supporter of the entrepreneurial community.